ANTHOLOGY
OF
CLASSIC
ARTICLES

The Christian Science Publishing Society
One Norway Street, Boston, Massachusetts 02115 U.S.A.

Anthology of Classic Articles

ISBN-13: 978-0-87510-421-8
ISBN-10: 0-87510-421-5

Printed in USA

PUR0801005

Table of Contents

INDEXES

INTRODUCTION

This *Anthology of Classic Articles* is a compilation of inspiring and uplifting essays about God and His loving relationship with each one of us. These articles were drawn from the more than 50,000 published in *The Christian Science Journal* and the *Christian Science Sentinel* between 1908 and 1981. They were selected with the help of a group of Christian Science teachers and practitioners, who cited these articles as being especially valuable in the healing practice.

Mary Baker Eddy, the Discoverer and Founder of Christian Science, started the monthly *Journal* in 1883, and the weekly *Sentinel* in 1898, to help proclaim the message that spiritual laws of healing, as practiced by Christ Jesus, are forever accessible to humanity. For more than 100 years these magazines have documented effective spiritual healing as demonstrated by Christian Scientists. This *Anthology* represents a step in making the resources from past issues of the magazines more broadly available.

In the back of this collection you'll find indexes of subjects, authors, and publication dates, as well as more information about Mary Baker Eddy and her book *Science and Health with Key to the Scriptures*. To subscribe to current issues of *The Christian Science Journal* and the *Christian Science Sentinel*, or to purchase a copy of *Science and Health*, please visit *www.spirituality.com*, or call 617-450-2000. To learn more about Christian Science, please visit *www.christianscience.com* or your local Christian Science Reading Room.

The Christian Science Publishing Society

THE ACTIVITY OF THE CHRIST

*S*ome time ago the writer stood on the deck of a ship in the wee small hours of the morning. The stars hung low in the tropical sky, and on the horizon a lighthouse flashed its welcome. We were approaching land. Then came the dawn gradually, gradually, until the sky was aflame with glory.

To the writer, that dawn symbolized the activity of the Christ. Before it darkness fled. As she watched, there came an overwhelming sense of the magnitude of what was going on. Nothing could stop the dawn, because it was impelled by the power which governs the universe, a power which the world cannot touch.

"Why," she thought, "if all mankind—every man, woman, and child of every race and creed—were leagued together to prevent this dawn, if all the diabolical inventions of physical force and nuclear weapons, of human hate and mesmeric control, were hurled against it, they would not even touch it, much less stop it, for the power which governs the universe is God."

In the familiar opening verses of the Gospel of John we read (1:1, 3): "In the beginning was the Word, and the Word was with God, and the Word was God. . . . All things were made by him; and without him was not any thing made that was made." The Word is God's self-revealing activity, which, like the dawn, cannot be hindered or stopped.

The intelligent activity whereby Soul reveals its vastness, glory, and beauty is the Christ. And this intelligent activity or reflection is God's infinite knowing, whereby God, Soul, reflects Himself in untold splendor and glory. Whatever Mind, God, knows and is conscious of is the Christ, His infinite manifestation, and this manifestation is Truth. Thus in the Science of Mind, the knower, the knowing, and the known are one in being. There is no division or separation between God and His manifestation.

The Christ, then, shows forth God's infinite knowing—the glory of spiritual being, the radiance of spiritual might. The Christ is instantaneous. It does not need time to make itself felt. The Christ is always present, always active, always potent, always complete. That which the Christ reveals is itself, God's perfect manifestation. Thus in healing the sick and the sinning, the Christ demonstrates the fundamental facts that harmony has never been lost, that discord has never been real, and that perfection has never been impaired.

How divinely natural is this action of the Christ, this compelling power of divine Love! There is nothing labored, nothing harsh, nothing arduous or toilsome about it. Like the dawn, the action of the Christ is inviolate. It is incapable of being reversed or hindered by the supposititious onslaughts of evil.

The prophet Isaiah wrote (9:2), "The people that walked in darkness have seen a great light: they that dwell in the land of the shadow of death, upon them hath the light shined." Mary Baker Eddy says in the Christian Science textbook, *Science and Health with Key to the Scriptures* (p. 504), "The rays of infinite Truth, when gathered into the focus of ideas, bring light instantaneously, whereas a thousand years of human doctrines, hypotheses, and vague conjectures emit no such effulgence."

The irresistible Christ is the power of Mind. There is no healing, no redemption, no salvation but by this power. Healing, redemption, and salvation are not in matter. The power of Mind is the Messiah, and salvation depends upon the demonstration of God as the Mind of man. The Christ, Truth, must be lived and practiced, not theorized about.

There is no deliverance from material sense so long as we think of ourselves as frail, finite objects living in a big extraneous world, a belief which is fraught with fear and helplessness. One of the fundamental facts of the Science of Soul is that Mind, or Principle, is not in its idea; but idea is forever in Mind, and Mind is the one and only Ego. Thus individual spiritual man is not a separate, finite ego, as personal sense would have us believe. He exists to glorify God, and he reflects or expresses the eternal, infinite individuality or Mind, which includes within itself every expression of God, from the least to the greatest.

Physical sense is rank mesmerism. The physical senses are diametrically opposed to spiritual truth. They do not acknowledge the allness of Mind, and consequently they do not comprehend the subjective nature of being. Physical sense says that you are a person surrounded by other persons who dominate and control your life; that you live as a tiny speck in an immense world outside of yourself, a world of forces and circumstances which you do not understand and over which you have no control. We cannot fit Christian Science into this pattern or demonstrate its unerring Principle from this basis.

Christian Science reveals the allness of Mind. It shows us that things are not what they appear to be; that the person who is blocking our progress, the circumstance which is crushing out our health, the frustration which is robbing us of joy, are aggressive mental suggestions, not physical conditions—aggressive suggestions arguing that God is not All and that there is something beside Him.

No matter what form error may assume, through Christian Science we can reject it as unreal and illegitimate. We can dismiss it as a suggestion which cannot tempt us because God, the Mind of man, knows it not. God's idea, man, is as incapable of experiencing discord, sin, or limitation as is God Himself. Christ Jesus, our Way-shower and Master, proved this for the salvation of all mankind.

The Christ is the presence of the power of God and the power of the presence of God. The Christ is never static. The manifestation of God's functioning presence, which is the Christ, never ceases. It is never congested; it is never confused, obscured, obstructed; nor can it ever be reversed. It never comes to an end, never overworks, never wavers, never stops. Thus being never grows old; it never wears out; intelligence never lapses into senility and disease; Love never changes into hate; Life never ends in death. The Christ, God's divine power and action, is present under all circumstances, at all times, in all conditions. The Christ is law to every situation.

Jesus demonstrated the Christ as man's spiritual selfhood. Mrs. Eddy says (*Science and Health*, p. 482), "Jesus was the highest human concept of the perfect man." He was the highest human concept of the Christ. We have only to study thoughtfully the chapter entitled "Glossary" in the textbook to see that the Biblical characters there defined are all of them but human concepts of man, the divine idea.

For example, Abraham exemplifies the Christly attribute of fidelity; Asher, hope and faith. Dan presents an inverted concept of man, which is animal magnetism and has in it no element whatsoever of the Christ. Jesus is the truest and highest human concept, the one which more than all others presents the Christ.

So you and I as persons, and all the persons who form our universe—friends, family, fellow church members, world dictators, and others—are human concepts of the real man, the Christ, concepts evolved by the so-called human mind. As through the Science of Christ the human mind yields to the divine Mind, the human concept improves until it finally disappears in the radiance of God's likeness. Man's individuality and identity, being wholly spiritual, exist apart from materiality and are always intact and complete.

Mortal belief says that each person is the result of a long, long line of human ancestry and that in him are epitomized the traits and frailties of generations of forebears. But Christian Science, through its revelation of the Christ, enables us to commute the mesmeric sentence of personal sense; to banish the bondage of heredity, and to claim the reality and royalty of our being in Spirit.

Jesus consistently identified himself as the Christ, the Son of God. He acknowledged God as his Father and repudiated the ties of the flesh. In him the mesmerism of sensuous generation was broken. Jesus never swerved from the divinity of his origin. He demonstrated the Science of creation. His sense of himself was wholly spiritual. He spoke of himself as coming down from heaven, yet being in heaven (see John 3:13), and he submitted, according to the material senses, to the crucifixion to prove to mankind the eternality of Life and the way of escape from death. Standing before Pilate, in his supreme moment of mockery and trial, Jesus said (John 19:11), "Thou couldest have no power at all against me, except it were given thee from above." In claiming the divinity of his origin, he demonstrated the divinity of his destiny.

In a passage of sublime promise, Mrs. Eddy writes in *The First Church of Christ, Scientist, and Miscellany* (p. 119): "Mary of old wept because she *stooped down* and looked into the sepulchre—looked for the person, instead of the Principle that reveals Christ. The Mary of to-day looks up for Christ, away from the supposedly crucified to the ascended Christ, to the Truth that 'healeth all thy diseases' and gives dominion over all the earth."

It was the Christ, the spiritual idea, that appeared to human consciousness as the man Jesus. It is the Christ that appears to human consciousness today as Science. If we would find our individuality and identity and the individuality and identity of our loved ones, we must not stoop down and look into the sepulcher of personal sense. We must look up and let Science reveal the spiritual nature of man and the universe.

All that ever has existed is God and His Christ, God and His idea. In reality there never has been a human concept, for the human mind has never projected aught that is real. Christian Science enables us to reverse material sense testimony at every point and free ourselves from the bondage of materiality.

Crucifixion, resurrection, and ascension, birth, death, and all that appears to go on between these points belong to the human concept. The Christ is not resurrected, nor has it ever ascended. It exists as ever-presence and abides in the Mind of God. The Christ is forever at the standpoint of perfection.

Consciousness is never on a cross or in a tomb, nor does spiritual consciousness include a cross or a tomb. Mind's conscious existence is as incapable of being impaired as is the dawn. It forever includes only the things of God, of eternal Life and everlasting Love. Jesus' triumph over death shows us our present immortality.

Throughout his ministry Jesus demonstrated the coexistence of God and man. His assurance of the immortality of the Christ included his assurance of the preexistence of the Christ. He knew it to be impossible for Life ever to have had a beginning. Had Life ever begun, it would have to end. The continuity of existence and of identity is never interrupted by birth or death, nor do existence and identity pass through the vicissitudes of so-called material life.

Jesus understood this. He understood Life and being to be above and beyond all finite sense of existence. He knew that every manifestation of Life evidences the one Ego expressing itself, and is timeless, ageless, deathless, eternal. He demonstrated Life in the fullness of its glory. He knew that the one Spirit, or Soul, includes the beauty and variety of form, outline, color of all that Spirit, Soul, reflects, includes the Christ in its full-orbed glory and radiance.

Through self-purification and spiritual growth, we must demonstrate the Christ as did the Master. We must be able to say with Paul (II Cor. 5:16), "Henceforth know we no man after the flesh: yea, though we have known Christ after the flesh, yet now henceforth know we him no more." In the

radiance of God's self-revealing activity, which is Science, we demonstrate the Christ as the presence of the power of God and the power of the presence of God, and man in God's likeness shines forth.

—*L. Ivimy Gwalter*

AGELESS BEING

"Can there be any birth or death for man, the spiritual image and likeness of God?" Mary Baker Eddy asks this question on page 206 of *Science and Health with Key to the Scriptures.* The belief of age, including birth, growth, maturity, and decline, rests on a false material concept of man. The understanding of man's true status replaces this false concept with proof of man's unchanging spiritual birthright. Christian Science gives us this understanding. It teaches us that the years do not bring changes or increase age; only false belief, which is subject to correction, does this. We learn through Science that man is indeed the image and likeness of God, ageless and immortal; and we learn that by accepting and living this truth, we can prove it in our daily lives.

Christ Jesus realized eternal life. He said (John 8:58), "Before Abraham was, I am," and he proved man's eternality visibly to Peter, James, and John. The Bible relates that he was transfigured before them. We read also (Matt. 17:3), "There appeared unto them Moses and Elias talking with him." Jesus was our Way-shower. He knew God as the Life of man; therefore he knew man as the very expression of eternal Life. He knew the grandeur of man, the newness of man in the likeness of God, and he knew that any appearance of mortality was completely deceptive. He brought forth proof that man reflects or shows forth the ageless being of God.

In our day-by-day human experience, until we begin to awake to the Christly sense of man that Jesus gave us, we often allow ourselves to be fooled by material thinking. We believe in the process of growing from childhood to manhood and then from manhood declining toward death, and we believe that each birthday adds another year toward this end.

Christian Science shows us that in estimating what is real, our task is to separate material beliefs from spiritual facts. We must establish in our thinking the spiritual fact that God is All-in-all, always present, and that man is His perfect reflection. We see that our prayer, as well as our work in Christian Science, is primarily to awaken to man's real selfhood in God. Our recognition of God's presence and our acceptance of and trust in the truth of being bring healing and release from every ill, including the handicaps of age; because the quality of our thinking determines our outward human experience, and spiritual thinking has behind it the power of God.

In *Science and Health* Mrs. Eddy says (p. 244), "Man in Science is neither young nor old." On the next page she tells of a woman who, disappointed in love at an early age, became insane and did not notice the passing years. When she was seventy-four, some travelers who saw her believed that she was still a young woman. Mrs. Eddy adds, "One instance like the foregoing proves it possible to be young at seventy-four; and the primary of that illustration makes it plain that decrepitude is not according to law, nor is it a necessity of nature, but an illusion."

A member of my family had a wonderful proof of God's power over the belief of age. He was employed by a large corporation, and although he was a valuable worker, about eight years ago he had to conform to the company's rule and retire. He had no special interest apart from his work; this meant that he was soon doing nothing and was manifesting all the common symptoms of age. He seemed to be in a daze; he could not think clearly or remember. Sometimes he would lose consciousness.

Through treatment in Christian Science he was healed and went to work in a new position. Today his thought is clear and free, and he is in good health. He reads the Bible Lesson in the *Christian Science Quarterly* every morning before he goes to work and acknowledges that he is in reality God's perfect child. He says he has learned to pray by thanking God for all good; whereas in the past he would plead with God and ask Him for things he thought he should have. He has learned in Christian Science that God gives us what we need, because man always exists in reality as the perfect reflection or manifestation of God.

Man's real selfhood is ever at one with God, and we claim and prove this selfhood by knowing the truth of man in God's likeness. Since Mrs. Eddy gave *Science and Health* to the world, longevity has increased. The revelation of God as All-in-all and of man in God's likeness enables one to rely on God with confidence and to trust His guidance in human affairs.

In the light of this revelation, we can learn to live one day at a time and to have no doubt that God takes care of our future. We see, indeed, that we have something far more wonderful than a future—we have ageless being. Our work is to view existence from the standpoint of immortality and to bring out daily proofs of the words of the Apostle John in the Bible (I John 3:2), "Beloved, now are we the sons of God."

—Juliet Rothschild

ALL THE WAY

The one all-inclusive God can never know frustration or inactivity. Deity being omniactive Life, His creation cannot become stagnant, but must be rightly active. It consists of spiritual ideas, which abide in divine Mind and are forever unfolding harmoniously according to divine law. It would be impossible for God to create ideas that were deficient or capable of functioning imperfectly. The understanding that Love constantly controls and eternally provides for its ideas can be applied daily.

More than thirty-five years ago the employees of the old Boston Elevated Railway Company were on strike. Two friends of the writer's who needed to go downtown to the courthouse started to walk in from the outskirts. On their way a chauffeur stopped his car to offer them a ride. He was not going downtown he explained—only halfway—but would be glad to take them that distance. The husband answered that they would be happy to accept.

His wife said nothing but thought: "Love never takes anyone halfway. Love takes us all the way." Immediately she recognized this as an angel message and said, "Thank You, Father; that's all I need." While she was gratefully pondering the spiritual fact that Love's purpose is always fully accomplished, that the Father glorifies the son completely, that in any situation, whatever stems from Principle is finished by Principle, the chauffeur called out, "This is halfway, but I have time to take you all the way and would be glad to do so."

Of course her demonstration was not in being taken to the courthouse, but in discerning and accepting a spiritual truth. Ever since that time she has often used the truth, "Love takes us all the way." When a case of sickness has improved, she has realized that Love not only makes one better, but also heals completely. When error has argued that retrenchment was necessary, she has known that Love does not partially meet one's needs, but bestows on man the infinite resources of Soul. When facing tasks that seemed beyond her, she has recalled that divine intelligence never furnishes the opportunity for a service without giving one the ability with which to perform it. Love supports whatever is constructive in our experience. Love never uncovers a selfish material tendency without supplying the unselfishness and spirituality which annihilate it. "Love takes us all the way."

Can anyone picture Jesus as believing in frustration? Then if we follow our Master, we shall not admit that God does things halfway. God does not give us a right desire and then fail to bring it to fruition. There is not a partially consummated or fruitless transaction in God's plan for His creation. As we read in the book of Zechariah (8:12), "The seed shall be prosperous; the vine shall give her fruit, and the ground shall give her increase, and the heavens shall give their dew; and I will cause the remnant of this people to possess all these things."

Even when mortal mind argues retrogression in an experience or aggravation of an illness, mental chemicalization or the action of Truth in human consciousness is merely bringing evil to the surface to be destroyed. Love's law alone is operating to the end of producing harmony. Nor does Love heal for a time. Love's healing is forever. God eternally maintains man in His likeness. Therefore one can never manifest what error falsely claims he once had. Again, there will be no frustration in our experience if we become a law unto ourselves and refuse to acquiesce in evil's argument that God does things part way. Let us rather accept the law of Love as the law governing us completely.

Man, God's idea, is never separated from but abides in Mind. He is not a material personality in a discordant situation from which he needs to be extricated; his individuality is completely spiritual. Mary Baker Eddy writes (*Miscellaneous Writings*, p. 310), "To impersonalize scientifically the material sense of existence—rather than cling to personality—is the lesson of to-day." The relinquishment of the false belief that a problem, whether sickness or frustration, is personal, and the recognition that it is an illusion in an impersonal, false sense, aids in demonstrating man's flawless spiritual individuality.

The truth necessary to solve every problem is present where the problem seems to be. This truth is already known to infinite, all-knowing Mind and to man, Mind's reflection. It cannot be hidden. Moreover, Love makes it evident to our thought and in our experience. Isaiah thus portrayed God's law of inevitable fruition (Isa. 65:21, 22): "They shall build houses, and inhabit them; and they shall plant vineyards, and eat the fruit of them. They shall not build, and another inhabit; they shall not plant, and another eat: for as the days of a tree are the days of my people, and mine elect shall long enjoy the work of their hands." Fruition and accomplishment are not something outside the real man he needs to get. They are inherent in his being. He forever possesses them because he includes all the right ideas and attributes of God.

Failing to grasp the real man's spiritual nature and present perfection, mankind believes man is material, therefore subject to limitation and frustration. When a right purpose seems thwarted, it is wont to exclaim, "Another one of those things!" This expression implies that some uncontrollable evil influence exists and has acted against man's well-being. Error's false claim should be denied, not admitted. In so far as an experience is limiting or harmful it is untrue, hence not going on in God's harmonious universe.

In Science there are none of "those things," nothing that has functioned or can work against man's perfection. God's law, the law of good, alone is operating, and it forever blesses man. God's will is, has been, and always will be done. In reality the answer to every prayer and the fulfillment of every right desire are in Mind. Let us say so with no mental reservation and obtain the benison always redounding to those who completely acknowledge God.

Because human experience is entirely subjective —the externalization of human thought—it can be improved as thought is spiritualized. Mrs. Eddy declares in *Science and Health with Key to the Scriptures* (p. 403), "You command the situation if you understand that mortal existence is a state of self-deception and not the truth of being." What appears as failure or frustration is a state of self-deception. Only as we are willing to admit this are we in a mental position to "command the situation" and nullify mortal mind's claim to hinder any righteous endeavor.

And we shall find that a demonstration in Christian Science has a twofold significance. It increases our gratitude for God's allness and perfection and spurs us on to greater achievements Spiritward. As Thomas Huxley wrote, "The rung of a ladder was never meant to rest upon, but only to hold a man's foot long enough to enable him to put the other somewhat higher." Problems met and mastered enable us to rise higher in our demonstration of reality. Then we prove practical God's promise (Ex. 31:3), "And I have filled him with the spirit of God, in wisdom, and in understanding, and in knowledge, and in all manner of workmanship." It is the promise that we

are filled "with the spirit of God, . . . in all manner of workmanship" that mankind should unfailingly appropriate.

Duties will not seem burdensome if we understandingly claim the spontaneity and joy inherent in man as the blessed child of God. Stagnation will be ruled out of our affairs as we accept, despite sense testimony, the spiritual fact that progress, God's unopposable law of the unfoldment of good, is ever operative in man's experience. Indeed, one can refuse to be deluded into believing that the expression of Principle can ever fail to be secure, joyous, rightly active, or justly rewarded.

Not only in our duties but when error suggests illness or duress, Love is present to deliver. If an individual fell over an embankment or into a deep abandoned well, his companion would not just throw him a rope. His friend would encourage him to hang on, assuring him that he would be pulled to safety. The one in need would be made to feel that behind that rope were the strength and intelligence of his rescuer.

Sometimes, during a sorrow or an illness, error may argue that there is nothing we can do. Yet we can hang on to the rope—that is, keep active in our consciousness the right idea which Love provides. It will always be our savior. Why? Because, as our Leader tells us (*Science and Health*, p. 6), "God is not separate from the wisdom He bestows."

The thoughts God gives are not partly effective, nor are they ever separated from Deity. On the contrary, they carry with them His intelligence, action, and power; in fact, everything necessary for their unfoldment and fruition.

The inspiration of divine Mind makes an untoward experience or illness so unreal that we see it was never any part of man. Love not only heals; it wipes out every vestige of sickness and remembrance of sin.

If we feel that a healing is delayed, or that we are up against an apparent wall of frustration, we can rejoice to find that, because of the revelation of Christian Science, God's law cannot be abrogated. Evil is forever unreal. In every situation Love is present to act quickly and conclusively, to "take us all the way."

Indeed, we have the same inspiration and conviction that enabled the Psalmist to record for humanity the complete, unassailable operation of the law of Love when he wrote, "I will cry unto God most high; unto God that performeth all things for me" (Ps. 57:2).

—*Milton Simon*

"As birds flying"

"As birds flying, so will the Lord of hosts defend Jerusalem; defending also he will deliver it; and passing over he will preserve it." This inspiring description of true defense given in the thirty-first chapter of Isaiah illustrates the manner in which Truth defends the citadel of each individual consciousness. Through Christian Science a spiritual realm of ideas is revealed where thought soars joyous, fearless, and free, expressing or reflecting the dominion, the power, and the presence of divine Love, or Principle. Mary Baker Eddy writes in the Christian Science textbook, *Science and Health with Key to the Scriptures*, under the marginal heading "Soaring aspirations" (pp. 511–512), "The fowls, which fly above the earth in the open firmament of heaven, correspond to aspirations soaring beyond and above corporeality to the understanding of the incorporeal and divine Principle, Love." These soaring aspirations which fly in "the open firmament of heaven," in "the understanding of the incorporeal and divine Principle, Love," are truly our defense, for they are conscious only of the perfection and presence, the harmony and happiness, of divine being.

Defense is not merely a state of resistance to error; it detects and attacks with the consciousness of good's allness any claim to existence, power, or presence apart from Truth. True defense is an active state of thought which utilizes and expresses ideas of Mind by proving the allness and ever-presence of divine Principle, God, and the consequent nothingness of all unprincipled beliefs. To attempt to detect and destroy error by remaining on the level which believes in its reality, and merely denying this belief, will not prove the all-power and all-presence of God. Every valid denial of evil is based on the understanding of the perfection of God and of man as God's likeness. To attempt to rid oneself of erroneous thoughts through suppression or through evasion, while still believing in the reality of evil and in its disastrous results, may seem to bring temporary freedom but leaves a vacuity in human consciousness that consequently invites more errors to lodge within it.

Jesus described this state of thought in the parable of the unclean spirit that left a man and went forth through desert places and, unable to find a resting place, returned to its original abode and found the man's consciousness empty, "swept and garnished." Then the unclean spirit sought seven other evil spirits or beliefs worse than itself and they dwelt there, so that the last state of that man was worse than the first (see Luke 11:24–26). This is not the defense which dislodges and destroys error through the knowing of the all-presence of Truth and its ideas. True defense is experienced by that consciousness which is filled with the realization of the ever-present, ever-active nature of Principle, Truth, and Love. Truth's defense lies in knowledge of its eternal, indestructible, self-existent nature, for Truth is the eternal reality of all being.

Should a person be in a prison camp, under the domination of an enemy nation, in bondage to sickness, fear, or lack, he will find that his defense against these conditions lies in soaring aspirations which rise "beyond and above corporeality to the understanding of the incorporeal and divine Principle, Love." To recognize the presence of Love where hate may seem to be; to behold the omnipotence of good where the forces of evil and disease claim to hold sway; to declare the government of Principle with its justice, integrity, and love where injustice, tyranny, and cruelty seem to be in the ascendancy—in other words, to think the positive truth when erroneous suggestions seem prevalent—is true defense.

Mrs. Eddy uses the verbs defend, protect, and guard with discriminating understanding of their meaning. In her *Manual of The Mother Church* is the following By-Law (Art. VIII, Sect. 6): "It shall be the duty of every member of this Church to defend himself daily against aggressive mental suggestion, and not be made to forget nor to neglect his duty to God, to his Leader, and to mankind." In this By-Law it is plain that we do not need to defend ourselves against persons, places, conditions, or nations, but against suggestions, which have no truth, no value, no substance. These suggestions are so aggressive that they even claim to be our own thinking, surroundings, conditions, relationships, our home, our business, and our church. To recognize these discordant states as aggressive suggestions, never as persons, places, or things, or as our own thoughts, and to realize the presence of the thoughts and ideas of divine Principle, Love, as the real and only condition of being, is true defense.

A dictionary makes a clear distinction between the verbs defend, protect, and guard, with the following illustration: "The inmates of a fortress are *defended* by its guns, *protected* by its walls, and *guarded* by sentries." A gun is active. It shoots forth its charge, attacking that which is inimical to the preservation of the fortress. In military circles it is axiomatic that attack is often the best defense. Our Leader confirms this in her book *Retrospection and Introspection* where she states (p. 63), "We attack the sinner's belief in the pleasure of sin, *alias* the reality of sin, which makes him a sinner, in order to destroy this belief and save him from sin; and we attack the belief of the sick in the reality of sickness, in order to heal them." Our defense then is in attacking error by sending forth, expressing, or reflecting the truth of God and man, of God's allness, omnipotence, and ever-presence, which eliminates utterly error's claim to existence, presence, or power.

To continue with our simile of the guns which attack and destroy, we as Christian Scientists need to attack and destroy the enemy, which is never a person but always the mesmeric suggestion of defeatism, fear, discouragement, hatred, injustice, envy, or revenge, by recognizing Truth and Love as the only reality, even where error claims to have place and power. If the aggressive mental suggestion presents itself to us that we are being hated, we need to defend ourselves by knowing the truth that there is in reality no hatred and that, as God's ideas, we are being loved, for divine Love is everywhere present and is being expressed by all its creation. Thus man is eternally the recipient and expression of Love and feels its safety, comfort, inspiration, light, and joy.

Nowhere in her published writings does Mrs. Eddy use the phrase "protective work," but she does exhort us to *defend* ourselves, our church, and our Cause. The thought of protection generally implies that there is some evil from which one needs to be protected, whereas the thought of defense implies an active expression of worth, nobility, purity, truth, or goodness, which by its very nature repels and destroys all that is opposed to itself. In Science our *defense* lies in demonstrating the fact that divine Truth and Love are omnipotent, omnipresent, and omniactive, and that error, or evil, has therefore no power, existence, or action. Our *protection* consists of abiding under the shadow, or in the active reflection, of divine Love. We *guard* our citadel of consciousness by sentry duty which analyzes every thought that presents itself, asking its name or nature and not permitting its entrance unless it is known to be good, intelligent, pure, and upright.

Twice a year Christian Scientists study in the *Christian Science Quarterly* a Lesson-Sermon entitled "Ancient and Modern Necromancy, *alias* Mesmerism and Hypnotism, Denounced." One of the meanings of the word *denounce* is, "To proclaim, or give notice of, the termination of (a treaty, armistice, or the like)." There can be no treaty between Truth and error, no cessation of warfare, until Truth is proved to be victor. There can be no treaty between the armies of God's ideas and the hordes of aggressive mental suggestions which would try to deceive, mislead, enslave, through materialistic means and methods. This Lesson-Sermon makes clear the fact that it is not persons, nations, places, or conditions that we are to denounce, but the mesmerism or hypnotism which would have us fear, hate, envy, or destroy persons, nations, places, or things. A bird's defense against the mesmeric influence which a serpent may seem to exert over it is to fly upward into its own more ethereal atmosphere, where the serpent cannot follow. If the bird comes down to the earthy level of the serpent, its actions will be the result of mesmeric fear and not of intelligence.

The sixth chapter of II Kings describes the manner in which Elisha the prophet handled the mesmeric suggestion of warfare which the king of Syria was trying to wage against the king of Israel. Through his spiritual discernment Elisha was able to perceive the plans of the king of Syria and forewarn the king of Israel, so that the Syrians were never able to carry out their plans. The king of Syria discovered that it was Elisha who was affording this defense to Israel, and so he sent "horses, and chariots, and a great host" to surround the city of Dothan, where Elisha was dwelling. When Elisha's servant arose in the morning and saw the Syrian hosts surrounding his master and himself, he was mesmerized by fear.

Elisha, however, did nothing to disperse the army surrounding him; but he prayed that his servant's eyes might be opened to the exalted truth which he, the prophet, was perceiving, namely, that he was surrounded by the hosts of God's ideas, or by Love's angels. Then he proved that the army of Syria, governed by mesmeric suggestions, could not see him to take him captive; rather did he take this captivity of mesmeric materialism, force, or power captive by leading the Syrians into the camp of the Israelites. When the king of Israel asked the prophet if he should smite them, Elisha said that instead he should feed them and let them return to their master.

This is a clear example of the fact that the enemy is aggressive animal magnetism, or mesmerism, and not persons. Elisha did not hold it against the persons who were the instruments of animal magnetism, nor did he try to make a treaty or carry on a truce with the error. He proved the power of God, Mind, and His ideas to be victorious over the arguments of the material senses and their mesmeric suggestions. The outcome of the whole situation was that "the bands of Syria came no more into the land of Israel." Elisha's scientific handling of error's claims made it impossible for them ever to return.

It is the light of intelligence and love which makes clear to us error's claims and their nothingness. Therefore we need to rise to the realm of enlightened spiritual knowing in order to detect and destroy error in all its forms. A young naval aviator once related to a friend how difficult he had found it to obey the instructions to fly high in order to see deep into the ocean. In fact, he said, he was so convinced that this must be erroneous that he tried flying low over the water, but discovered he was much more aware of its density at a low level than when at a higher altitude, for from this latter altitude he was able to discern the penetration of the light into the water.

Those who have flown by airplane realize how much more comprehensive is their vision at high altitudes than when the plane is moving near the earth's surface. When the Christian Scientist needs to defend his thought against the aggressive mental suggestions of fear, envy, hatred, sin, sickness, and death, he rises through inspiration and revelation into the realm of spiritual understanding, from whence he can look deep into the sea of erroneous suggestion, detecting its intents and its utter powerlessness or nothingness. There has never been any error or erroneous suggestion in the realm of divine Truth and Love, where man lives and where thought soars upward, onward, and Godward.

Suggestions of discord, conflict, sin, disease, and death vanish as mists before the sun when thought soars in the consciousness of God's ability and power to preserve His own and in the realization that man reflects the self-existent I AM. Thus Christian Science reveals to us the inviolable, immutable, eternally perfect nature of man, who glorifies Soul by expressing its beauty and inspiration, who forever lives divine Life, who is the loving expression of divine Love, and who magnifies God as All.

O joy that ever will remain,
Midst seeming sorrow, hate, and pain,
Our hearts to fill with this glad song
That soars above the mists of wrong:
    Man is the loved of Love.

(*Christian Science Hymnal*, No. 232.)

—*Margaret Glenn Matters*

BEING IS
UNFOLDMENT

*E*veryone is naturally concerned with *being*—with what really is, as it pertains to himself and others; and when one considers the nature of being he sees that this is as it should be, for being is divine unfoldment, infinite Mind or divine Principle forever infinitely expressing itself according to its own unvarying perfection. The writings of Mary Baker Eddy make plain that the nature of being is unfoldment. Indeed she says (*Miscellaneous Writings*, p. 82), "Infinite progression is concrete being."

Unfoldment signifies a disclosing from within, the coming to light of something innate, indigenous, independent of external influence. It depends on native impulsion—on something inherent in that which unfolds. As understood in Christian Science, it is, in its absolute meaning, the immaculate nature of all that is, being expressed. This activity of divine Truth, discerned and demonstrated in human experience, supersedes and displaces false belief and brings greater harmony to humankind. That which is, unfolds, and this progress is manifest in human affairs when thought actively recognizes divine Mind as its source and rejects everything unlike Mind, thus bringing itself and its expression under divine Mind's law of unfoldment. Unfoldment must partake of the nature of infinity, because only infinity can express itself exhaustlessly.

Because infinity is, logic compels the acknowledgment that all there is to existence is eternally unfolding reality—infinite good ever appearing in obedience to its own infinite nature. This means that conscious, active, unfolding infinity or good is the only thing that is actually going on, or can go on. Because of its infinitude, real being excludes the possibility of anything outside of or unlike itself which can resist or obscure its spontaneous and satisfying evidence.

Unfoldment is divine Mind's mode of expression. It is Mind knowing and declaring itself. To humanity it appears either as the progressive revelation of reality in conscious individual experience, or as a crumbling of a false sense of what is good and desirable in order that thought may be turned from the false to the true. It is the activity of Love making divine facts manifest in human affairs; it is the showing forth, to human sense, of what is actually and continuously taking place.

It must be seen that divine unfoldment takes place as oneness, as allness. It cannot be going on here and not there; nor can it mean that "this" unfolds and "that" does not. Divine progress is universal as well as individual. It is each unfolding with all, and all unfolding with each. There is no private unfoldment, because Mind, God, is one and all, and unfolding infinity necessarily includes and blesses all. Opinionatedness, obstinacy, pride of accomplishment or attainment, pride of circumstance and pride of priesthood, all give place to this divine, satisfying unfoldment when one accepts it. Divine unfoldment includes all that can truly satisfy the ambition of the human intellect or the aspiration of the human heart; but these must first be held in abeyance and Truth sought for its own sake before satisfaction can be realized.

Unfoldment signifies infinity infinitely expressing itself forever, and its expression is infinite idea, or man, or universe. It is man's real, eternal experience, the only true experience that one can ever have. Nothing can be more specific than Mrs. Eddy's statement of this already quoted, "Infinite progression is concrete being." There is nothing that helps one more to put off fear, and to demonstrate an even, uncritical love of one's fellows, than a correct and continuous appreciation of what this means.

A right apprehension of infinity and its all-inclusive, universal activity, by showing the futility of mere human will and undemonstrated human effort, destroys a false sense of responsibility, and so relieves tension. It strengthens courage and expectation of good. It simplifies obedience to the Scriptural admonition and assurance, "In all thy ways acknowledge him, and he shall direct thy paths." Unfoldment reveals the simplicity of pure being, and thus begins to do away with the complexities and anxieties of mortal belief.

In the measure that one grasps the fact that God is Principle, and that this Principle is Love, he begins to see that all that is taking place or can take place is progressive good, and as a result his fears for the future and for his loved ones diminish noticeably. He has the assurance that the spiritual unfoldment which brings error to light will at the same time outshine the error. He perceives that what appears is either unfolding Truth or else some phase of error brought to light by Truth in order that Truth may dissipate it; and therefore increase of good and decrease of evil naturally characterize his human experience. Divine unfoldment is intelligence unfolding, Love unfolding, Life unfolding; and when accepted and affirmed as one's own thinking, it shows itself in greater health, happiness, and supply.

It must have been a steadfast conviction that being is unfoldment which enabled Jesus, in the face of insistent testimony to the reality of evil, to stand fearlessly and faithfully for man's perfection. He turned his attention from false presentations of personal sense to the certainty of harmonious facts and their progressive appearing. Following his example, a Christian Scientist is enabled to remain unmoved by the various phases error assumes to discourage him—sometimes on the very threshold of victory—and to continue in such assurance of the nature of unfailing good that demonstration follows. Indeed, Mrs. Eddy says in our textbook that "Jesus' demonstrations sift the chaff from the wheat, and unfold the unity and the reality of good, the unreality, the nothingness, of evil" (*Science and Health with Key to the Scriptures*, p. 269). Discouragement cannot long exist where the true nature of being is recognized, for then the inevitability of progress is seen, although, as with deep-rooted vegetation, the progress may not be immediately visible on the surface.

The understanding of Mind's unfoldment acts as the presence and power of Mind itself, because only Mind can know and evidence Mind's nature. Paul queries, "What man knoweth the things of a man, save the spirit of man which is in him? even so the things of God knoweth no man, but the Spirit of God" (I Cor. 2:11). The truths included in Mind are known, not to mortal mind, but to the thought which understands and approximates the divine Mind.

Divine unfoldment, or "infinite progression," is not something outside of consciousness. It is consciousness. It is subjective, and is expressed in one's own knowing and being. Until Science is revealed in individual consciousness, indeed as individual consciousness, not as theory or something external to one's identity, it is not apparent that goodness, power, immortality are native to man. Only in proportion as one claims his true identity does he find these qualities belonging to him, and to all men.

Perceiving unfoldment as the true nature of all being begins to do away with resistance, opposition, habitual unwillingness, fear, anxiety, uncertainty, and therefore to open the way for divine spontaneity to appear in one's thought and affairs. It is a practical encouragement and aid in all human endeavor. It

puts business on a firm foundation, for nothing can interfere with the success of a business or an enterprise scientifically seen as based in Mind, expressing Mind's unfoldment, and allowed to express it. Personal opinion, push, self-will, a humanly outlined procedure determinedly held to, all tend to obscure the harmonious action and evidence of Mind, and must be relinquished in order that satisfying progress may be manifest in one's daily affairs.

Jesus' feeding of the multitudes shows clearly the naturalness of unfoldment as Mind's mode of expression. Rejecting the personal sense presentation which blinded his disciples, he looked up to heaven, "the reign of Spirit; government by divine Principle," as heaven is scientifically defined in part in our textbook (*Science and Health*, p. 587). Thus recognizing all that exists as evidence of infinity, and therefore forever infinitely unfolding, he had the joy of witnessing his spiritual perception exemplified as unlimited human supply.

It would be well for all to recognize and rejoice at, as an evidence of unfolding infinity, everything big or little that comes in the way of good—of supply, or business, or occupation. Such an attitude of thought does much to release frozen assets, whether of opportunity, money, friendship, freedom, or health, and to keep one open to and receptive of good. When, therefore, one starts on a business trip or on a social or household errand, it is well to go not merely for the accomplishment of a limited end, but with thought open to anything in the way of good which may unfold.

It is worth reiterating that unfolding infinity is the whole of being, and this means not only that it is the only thing really going on, but that it is all that ever has gone on. Seeing this, one can redeem the past as well as the present, can regain the good of the years that have seemed full of mistakes. It shows that opportunity is ever present and ever available, and that scientifically there is no such thing as being too late for any good. Opportunity is not a momentary occasion, but a constantly unfolding idea.

Divine unfoldment is wholly good. Therefore every human being has the right to expect that, through true understanding, only good can come to him or to anyone. Likewise, he has the privilege of denying that he or another has ever, in reality, experienced evil, and of affirming and proving that good is and ever has been his only experience, and the only universal experience. In this way can be blotted out what appear to be present disturbances, because what human belief calls present is merely the outcome of what this same belief calls cumulative past. In the degree that one sees this, his thoughts become more uniformly good and impartially gracious, and he becomes a better friend, a more faithful, active citizen. He sees that good thinking, or thinking good, is the normal mental activity of every individual; that good constitutes the actual spiritual identity of everyone; and he experiences progressively the infinite unfolding of good.

Divine unfoldment is unfolding Truth, unfolding Mind, always kind, always beneficent. It is ever-satisfying Love in operation. Infinity, or being, necessarily unfolds infinitely forever. The whole of being is irresistible spiritual evolution. It includes all reality, all ideas, which are ever ceaselessly unfolding together. All unfolds as one, and each idea according to an unfailing, intelligent order. Let us, as Christian Scientists, learn to trust this unfoldment, to see that infinite unfoldment is inevitable, spontaneous; that it acts according to its own infinite momentum, and that it therefore connotes dominion.

—*Mary Sands Lee*

CAREERS

Success is defined in different ways in different societies. But whatever success is, according to our individual definition—being an effective business executive or welfare officer, or a prominent member of a respected profession or a productive scholar or an efficient homemaker—it is most fully achieved when built on a spiritual foundation. In Science, man is the idea of Life, God, always established in Life. The most successful career is the one based on reality—the scientific consciousness of man's present position in Life as Life's idea.

A successful career or lifework is a natural outcome of apprehending the reality of Life's immortal man and universe and making this the groundwork for the consistent work and self-discipline required. According to the Science of being reality is not that which is transmitted to us by the five personal senses. Christian Science challenges "consensus reality" (the seeming reality that human beings generally agree is *the* reality) on the ground that it is not authorized by infinite Truth, the only cause. Scientific reality is tangible to spiritual sense, the Spirit-derived capacity with which we are all equipped, though we may not be aware of it. "The manifestation of the Spirit," Paul points out, "is given to every man to profit withal" (I Cor. 12:7). There is no more satisfying career than developing spiritual sense. And there's no one who cannot find satisfaction and the peace of Mind on this basis.

So long as we think of ourselves as wholly immersed in matter and as pursuing a fully material career, our success is relatively limited and may be short-lived. Life in matter is a delusion. Science radically challenges the common view of life and purpose. Mrs. Eddy tells us, "Wholly apart from this mortal dream, this illusion and delusion of sense, Christian Science comes to reveal man as God's image, His idea, coexistent with Him—God giving all and man having all that God gives" (*The First Church of Christ, Scientist, and Miscellany*, p. 5).

The essence of a spiritual career is in giving up delusive dreams of corporeal living and inevitable dying and letting a spiritual sense of Life and man dawn on our thought. This opens out the infinite possibilities—the infinite actualities—of real being. Do you sometimes feel like a fruitlessly toiling mortal trying to carve for yourself a niche in what seems to be the hard granite of commerce or industry, the university, or a trade? Actually, you're the immortal expression of divine Life, already placed and classified in Life.

The metaphysical view of being is uniquely practical. Understanding our true self to be the expression of Life develops originality and integrity, foresight and stamina. When our thought has developed spiritual dimensions, we are less absorbed in the stresses and enigmas of mortality and more assured that Life's self-manifestation comprises our real identity and activities. We're more likely to make sound judgments, less likely to be anxious over career dilemmas.

Through Science we can find the tools with which to demonstrate divine Life. If we're young, this may mean finding and excelling in an appropriate career. If we're in midstream in life and dissatisfied or disappointed with our occupation, it means that we can begin to do better at it or perhaps embark on another. If we're retired and feeling unneeded, it means being able to find the activity we are best fitted to pursue, perhaps an activity of a kind we've never engaged in before and which we're uniquely qualified to do. The idea of Life is not governed by supposititious laws of age, which would impair faculties or limit opportunity and ability. Life's idea is always engaged in a spiritual career—being Life's expression—and includes the vitality and intelligence that derive from divine Life.

The career of Christ Jesus was entirely original and uniquely contributive to human welfare. He apprehended real being and purpose more fully than anyone before or since. His career points to the possibilities for us as we admit the Christ—the immortal truth of God and man—into our consciousness. Or, better, as we acknowledge that divine Life in its self-expression comprises our only genuine consciousness.

As Christian Science reveals to us realities before unseen, it unpacks opportunities for growth and healing previously unseen. The more conscious we are of the verities of divine being, the more consistently and effectively we heal physical and organizational ills. No matter how worthwhile the profession or trade we're in, Christian Science opens the way to what is fundamentally a healing career. This career is accessible to all of us, regardless of our lack or acquisition of degrees and diplomas.

Man as Life's idea does not live a life of material goals, of good and bad luck, of rewards and penalties, of competition and conflict, of financial success or failure. Man is the immortal evidence of Life's creativity, allness, and goodness. This is his career. There are not many careers, but one, and our genuine identity is even now occupied with it.

—*Geoffrey J. Barratt*

CHRIST JESUS AND TRUE SONSHIP

⁓

*T*he impact of the distinctive contribution Christ Jesus brought to mankind will be felt in human consciousness throughout time. He proved the full implication of man's sonship with God. He showed that true sonship originates in God.

It is natural for Christians everywhere to deepen and refresh their love for Jesus at Christmastime. They have an earnest desire to accord to him full credit for what he accomplished. Sometimes this sincere effort to recognize his unique place in history results in equating Jesus with God. To some it seems wholly inadequate to conceive of Jesus as simply a man. But to define Jesus as God would disguise the purpose of Jesus' presence on earth.

Jesus' life was not an illustration of how God could be manlike. Instead, his life afforded incontestable proof that man's true identity is Godlike. Jesus illustrated how each individual can realize himself to be the likeness of God. To define Jesus as God would misrepresent the nature of God, who is All, infinite Spirit.

On the other hand, to define Jesus' true nature as a mortal is to misrepresent his real identity. Jesus came not to show us that God can be a man but to disprove the belief that God's man is a mortal. He knew that man has a divine sonship with God. Ultimately his life revealed the full significance of true sonship. He understood that God was All—perfect Being—and that man's true sonship was the individual manifestation of God's nature. Man—the very expression of God's nature! What a wondrous heritage to be God's child—His son.

Jesus abundantly deserved the title "Christ." But he gave that term a meaning far beyond the identification of one man. His words and works showed that "Christ" is a term properly describing man's relationship to God—a pure sonship with God. The teachings of Christian Science explain that the Christ, as part of its broad and significant meaning to us, is the spiritual idea of true sonship (see *Science and Health with Key to the Scriptures,* p. 331).

The understanding of true sonship brought to mankind by Jesus is of profound significance to each of us today. The Christ, the true idea of sonship, defines the individual relationship we each have with God.

The concept of ourself as a mortal separates us, in belief, from God. An understanding of ourself as the son of God awakens us to our eternal unity with God. The Christ, this genuine essence of permanent sonship, isn't something that belongs to us as material persons. It is the enduring fact of being. The perfect and inseparable relationship between God and man can never be severed. Man's sonship with God is perpetual. Jesus didn't personally provide his fellowman with spiritual sonship. He brought to light the fact that, as God's man, they already had it. Mrs. Eddy poses the question, "Is man's spiritual sonship a personal gift to man, or is it the reality of his being, in divine Science?" In a statement affirming the latter, she says, "Man's knowledge of this grand verity gives him power to demonstrate his divine Principle, which in turn is requisite in order to understand his sonship, or unity with God, good" (*Miscellaneous Writings*, p. 181).

The clear recognition that man is born of God rather than of a mortal parentage has powerful implications. The birth of Jesus was an embarrassment—a profound affront—to materialistic beliefs about the nature of existence, and ultimately he refuted the entire concept that life is dependent on matter. His virgin birth set aside the so-called laws of nature and set the stage in human experience for final proof that God fathers man as a spiritual idea. His ascension brought fulfillment to his advancing proof that man's relationship to God is intact—that true sonship is undisturbed in the divine order of reality.

Each of us has the opportunity to grasp the spiritual sonship that we have with God. No one is excluded from this nature of the Christ. It is the Christ that reveals constant and uninterrupted sonship with God—it is the Christ that actually comprises our sonship with God. John tells us, "But as many as received him, to them gave he power to become the sons of God, even to them that believe on his name…" (John 1:12). To this powerful Bible promise, Mrs. Eddy brings spiritual insight: "His sonship, referred to in the text, is his spiritual relation to Deity: it is not, then, a personal gift, but is the order of divine Science" (*Miscellaneous Writings*, p. 181).

Jesus provided the supreme example of what it means to discover and live the Christ, this perfect, spiritual sonship. When an individual understands his true relationship to God, his life takes on fresh meaning. He no longer sees himself as bounded by mortal limitations. Man is the heir, even the expression, of Life and Love. Our lives can begin to be a prayer of affirmation proving man's spiritual sonship.

Man is not born of matter. He is the spiritual idea, the expression, of Spirit. Consciousness is the true substance of man's identity. What we term a material body is the supposed consciousness of limitation. Real being is the consciousness of spiritual sonship, an understanding that God and man are at one. The growing awareness of spiritual consciousness has a practical impact in our lives. It heals.

Jesus proved that the recognition of the Christ, divine sonship, enables us to exercise spiritual power. Material beliefs shrank before spiritual understanding. Every limitation of existence is based on the falsehood that our sonship is rooted in matter rather than Spirit. Those limitations—sin and illness, even death—begin to give way when, as Jesus taught, we look to Spirit as our Father. We find Christ to the extent we find our true relationship to God. Mrs. Eddy explains in *Science and Health*, "The real man being linked by Science to his Maker, mortals need only turn from sin and lose sight of mortal selfhood to find Christ, the real man and his relation to God, and to recognize the divine sonship" (p. 316).

What an unending debt of gratitude we owe Jesus—not just at the Christmas season, but throughout the year—for his demonstration of Christ. What he revealed of man's true relationship to God will eventually transform all of human consciousness. It will lift mankind out of the belief of life in matter and waken us to a very present fact—our full perfection as the sons of God.

—*Nathan A. Talbot*

THE CHRIST SCIENCE

⁓

In the latter part of the nineteenth century Christian Science was discovered by Mary Baker Eddy. During the first half of the twentieth century leading material scientists were breaking out of age-old concepts concerning matter and the so-called material universe; human thought was yielding to the eternal impetus of Truth. Mrs. Eddy's inspired discovery was pure Science, for in it were the tests of true wisdom, simplicity, and provability—the Science of the Christ, which the greatest Scientist who ever lived practiced in Galilee nearly two thousand years ago.

In the Gospel of St. John it is stated that if all the things Christ Jesus did were written, the whole world could not contain the books that would record them. What wealth of wisdom fell on dull ears and how long it has taken for the path of scholarly research to lead back to the Master's words! But now the world has arrived at that stage of spiritual progress where it can know and prove pure Science, the true idea of God, man, and the universe. From what vast horizons of spiritual vision must have arisen Jesus' utterance to his disciples (John 16:12, 13): "I have yet many things to say unto you, but ye cannot bear them now. Howbeit when he, the Spirit of truth, is come, he will guide you into all truth." Here is the prophecy that the fullness of wisdom must be the Science of Spirit, not of matter.

It is only as men sit at the feet of the master Metaphysician that they can learn true Science and support their understanding with evidence. Jesus brought to earth the knowledge that the universe is created spiritually, knowledge that existed before the beginning of time and that opened a vista of existence beyond the physical horizon. He did not explore the so-called realm of matter in the earth or in the heavens in order to explain the laws of creation, but spoke and worked from the knowledge which he had with God before the world was. He fathomed the work of God through the wisdom of God.

The Master's Science is undoubtedly the Science of eternity and infinity. Then it is not of human origin. It springs from foundational spiritual reality. It is not the result of human reason but of divine decree. Therefore it is to be approached from the standpoint of acceptance followed by demonstration, rather than through doubt and criticism, as is the method of the human mind when dealing with its theories of belief. The acceptance of divine Science wholeheartedly is not an offense against reason, nor is it arbitrary restriction of free thought. It is the opening of the mental window through which the illumination of Truth fills human consciousness with perfect understanding and power of demonstration.

Humanly developed so-called sciences are imperfect, changing, and chained to matter. They need the approach of skepticism and criticism in order to eliminate radical reliance on that which is not eternally true. The Science of God and of His universe is not to be questioned but practiced. It is not something to be argued about or experimented with, nor is it conventional reasoning or assumption. It is the pulsating presence of divine Love, unfolding the resources of the immeasurable. It is the Word of God, by which creation was formed and is forever unfolded. Aflame with the power of holiness, it reveals divine causation.

This pure Science demonstrates the reign of God with men, thus moving mankind toward paths of the infinite. As the true idea of being is embodied by mankind, this is the only direction in which they can move: toward the infinite and not toward an end; from the infinite and not from a beginning. The Discoverer and Founder of the Christ Science writes in her book *The First Church of Christ, Scientist, and Miscellany* (pp. 229–230), "Truth is strong with destiny; it takes life profoundly; it measures the infinite against the finite." How clearly this was illustrated in the life of the perfect Metaphysician, whose practice of divine Science took him from the helplessness of the cradle to the dominion of the ascension—from the finite to the infinite!

Consecrated study of the Science of the Christ, as epitomized in the life of the righteous Galilean, indicates that this Science is divine Principle's means of expressing itself throughout its universe of ideas. Acting with spiritual energy, Science deals with perfection; it is exact, imperative, supreme, endlessly unfolding the realities of immortal existence. All the laws of substance, Life, and intelligence belong to it, and all the elements, essence, and nature of being act in accord with it. As this divinely systematized knowledge gradually unfolds to the seeker, it is recognized as the only true Science there can be, because it is the Science of God, the All-in-all. It is understood to be the divine order of creator and creation, comprising the sum total of wisdom and demonstration.

As the student of divine Science passes from study to proof of spiritual wisdom, he becomes aware that the Science of Life is also the Science of Love, because it begins at once to bless him. In it there is not a single destructive element. Mistaken beliefs are corrected by it; what has seemed to be evil law is annulled; false dependencies no longer seem desirable; barriers to progress are removed; and daily answers to problems of human experience are worked out. The Science of living and loving as the Master taught it repeats its wonders of heaven now for him who obeys divine law.

Christian Scientists are progressing in the understanding of the energies of eternal Life and in demonstrating the use of this wisdom for the protection and salvation of mankind. As they realize the vast potentials in their field of spiritual discovery, their research and practice will fill and overflow the hours. Thus the knowledge of divine reality will be more speedily released to the human race. Such wisdom is powerful beyond human explanation—the atomic action of Mind delivering the whole earth from all seeming destructiveness of mortal belief. Christ Jesus gave an example of this truth when his tomb was opened to reveal man still living on, the master of death and the grave.

A penetrating paragraph on the subject of true atomic power, as part of the divine Science that performed the works of Jesus, is to be found on page 190 of Mrs. Eddy's *Miscellaneous Writings* and reads in this way: "Atomic action is Mind, not matter. It is neither the energy of matter, the result of organization, nor the outcome of life infused into matter: it is infinite Spirit, Truth, Life, defiant of error or matter. Divine Science demonstrates Mind as dispelling a false sense and giving the true sense of itself, God, and the universe; wherein the mortal evolves not the immortal, nor does the material ultimate in the spiritual; wherein man is coexistent with Mind, and is the recognized reflection of infinite Life and Love."

The close student of mathematics beginning with his numeration table catches glimpses of magnitudes and operations without end. His simplest calculation is always a prophecy of the great whole. As he uses the units of his science with infallible obedience to law, he arrives at the solution of every problem from the simplest to the most complex. In like manner the Christian

Scientist, yielding to divinely initiated unfoldment, will constantly be demonstrating the deeper interpretations of being. Mrs. Eddy writes in the *Message to The Mother Church for 1901* (p. 22), "I begin at the feet of Christ and with the numeration table of Christian Science." She goes on to say, "I adhere to my text, that one and one are two all the way up to the infinite calculus of the infinite God."

Because the master Metaphysician used the units of the Christ Science with perfect obedience to divine law, in the ascension he arrived at the supreme solution of eternal being. The primal order of man's spiritual sonship with God was demonstrated as changeless fact, and the seeming temporary disorder of materialism gave everlasting place to reality. He could impart only to a few any understanding of man's dominion over the whole earth, but he could trust that the time would come when the ears of humanity would be unstopped to hear the voice of Truth, explaining the way of eternal harmony. He said that his words would never pass away, and this prophecy is renewedly fulfilled in the coming of Christian Science.

Pure Science is as available through revelation to one as to another. Communion with God, not academic education, is the channel of its flowing to humanity. As it unfolds reality to mankind, pure Science embraces every step of progress within its own law, so that the ways of men may change from those of revolution to revelation. The Christ Science is still the way of resurrection, ascension, and immortality.

Christ Jesus' practice of divine Science was his reflection of God's intelligence. This is the only way whereby all men may cognize and demonstrate man's dominion over the earth. The discoveries of the sages have led to seeming magnified evil as well as to good. In the exploring of the transient realm of matter perils arise, and men may become victims of their own endeavors. In his delving into the spiritual realm, only the endless Science of divine harmony awaits the searcher. This experience delivers him at every point from the confines and dangers of a material sense of existence and opens the gates of progress that lead to eternal Life.

The Christ Science verifies the unreality of evil and the infinitude of divine reality. This Science permanently removes from human consciousness the false beliefs of life in matter by explaining the spirituality of the universe. It declares and proves that all power belongs to God—to Spirit, Mind,

Truth, Love, Principle—and that the functioning of this power is the reign of heaven.

Divine Science takes men beyond the mortal belief of earth and stars to the recognition of the kingdom of God within man and throughout the vastness of Mind. In the discovery of Christian Science the world has been given the answer to what has been called the riddle of the universe.

—Julia M. Johnston

CHURCH,
A LIVING POWER

Christian Science, the Science of Christianity as taught by the Master, Christ Jesus, is an irresistible power for good in today's distraught world.

What is it that binds its followers together and implements its forward thrust? Is it not the Church of Christ, Scientist? If those who wanted Christian Science had Mary Baker Eddy's book, *Science and Health with Key to the Scriptures*, but there were no church, these seekers for Truth would be scattered, rolling around in a sea of orthodoxy like isolated fragments. Mrs. Eddy saw that the founding of the church was integral to the revelation, and she saw that uniting with this church was not a one-time formal act but a continuing spiritual growth on the part of the individual.

So, just what is Church? We sometimes refer superficially to the little white spire on the village green or the stately buildings of The Mother Church as a beautiful church. But these are only symbols. To understand Church we must understand the spiritual idea that underlies the institution.

In the Glossary of *Science and Health* Mrs. Eddy opens her definition of *Church*: "The structure of Truth and Love; whatever rests upon and proceeds from divine Principle" (p. 583). Since Truth, Love, Principle, in Christian Science are synonymous with Mind, this definition lifts our sense of Church at once to the realm of infinite Mind, or divine consciousness, to Mind's cognizance of what is going on within itself. Man, as God's reflection, existing in Mind, can never exist apart from divine consciousness. Divine consciousness is our very being. We can never do without it. Indeed, we can never *be* without it. So we can never be without Church.

To say that we should see Church in this light is not to state a platitude; it is to perceive a truth that demands demonstration. Church, then, must be high in our list of priorities. We must love Church, cherish it, understand it. Unless we are demonstrating Church in our daily life, we are not demonstrating Christian Science, for Church is "whatever rests upon and proceeds from divine Principle."

Human thought is finite. It divides all things. We say, This is my church; this is my business, my home, my social life, my health, and so on. But in Science it is all one, one great active whole in spiritual consciousness, "the structure of Truth and Love."

Everything we do, everything we are, is inseparable from Church. Then it behooves us to get a truer concept of Church. And this comes through prayer, through deep study and pondering of the Bible and Mrs. Eddy's writings. This spiritual concept must be demonstrated in our love and devotion to church as we humanly perceive it. It must make us willing and eager to serve and give.

Nothing exists outside of consciousness, and everything real "rests upon and proceeds from divine Principle." So Church includes all creation singing praise to the creator. May this not be what the Master was pointing out when he said that "the true worshippers shall worship the Father in spirit and in truth"? (John 4:23).

The second paragraph in the Glossary definition of *Church* reads, "The Church is that institution, which affords proof of its utility and is found elevating the race, rousing the dormant understanding from material beliefs to the apprehension of spiritual ideas and the demonstration of divine Science, thereby casting out devils, or error, and healing the sick." This institution is not a separate church, a lesser church. It is the great truth of Church as divine idea made practical in human experience.

In this spiritual sense of structure each idea performs its own unique and useful function. Each church member, therefore, must know himself to be inseparable from the one great whole. He finds his usefulness as he individually demonstrates in his own life the oneness of Principle and its idea.

No one is out of place in this spiritual concept of Church, and no human manipulation is required to hold each in his proper sphere of activity. The need is for more active love reflected by all. In Christian Science we learn that in any seeming structural disruption, dislocation, or inharmony, whether in our bodies or in our church, the remedy is to establish in thought the spiritual sense of structure. As we demonstrate this spiritual sense, we take our proper place in church and its activity, and the blessing of this is experienced in the community and in every aspect of our lives. Nothing in God's infinite structure can ever be displaced, destroyed, or broken.

And this structure is not static. It is constantly growing, unfolding, multiplying, expanding, in accordance with God's plan of completeness, harmony, perfection. In proportion as we claim this truth for our church we will see it unfold in our lives. God's building never ceases. It neither starts nor stops, and it never deteriorates, grows old, or dies. This dynamic truth of Church as spiritual structure embraces our identity—our bodies, our faculties, our careers, our very reason for existing!

The function of Church is to heal—to destroy sin and end sickness. Every church service must heal because it is the voice of Truth, the Christ speaking to human consciousness, causing material misconceptions to yield. So Church becomes a living power in human lives. Is it not this dynamic truth that alone can feed the world's famine? As we recognize this, our love for Church grows, and more and more every business meeting of our branch church will become an inspiration meeting—a healing experience—alive with the Christ.

So Church is not a place of worship; it is a state of worship—a state of spiritual consciousness. Its walls are salvation; its gates are praise! Here in Love's outpouring of love we may find the son or dear one who has strayed. Here too we find our business, home, health—everything, embraced in harmony, purity, sinlessness, sufficiency.

It is significant that in the Middle Ages the one unjustly sentenced or persecuted, or the fugitive from justice, could flee into the church and find asylum there. So long as he remained in church he was safe. Today all may find safety in Church, not in a material edifice but in the spiritual idea. Did not the Master point to this when he said, "Upon this rock I will build my church; and the gates of hell shall not prevail against it"? (Matt. 16:18)

Mrs. Eddy's expansive love for humanity brought the Church of Christ, Scientist, into being. In her discovery, in the writing of *Science and Health*, in the founding of her Church, each unfolding step was characterized by healing, healing, healing.

Mrs. Eddy's concept of Church embraced the world. She saw:

- one Mother Church enfolding the world in its branches
- one worldwide membership
- one timeless impersonal pastor, the Bible and *Science and Health*
- one Lesson-Sermon [in the *Christian Science Quarterly*] studied the world over throughout the week by every Christian Scientist and delivered every Sunday in The Mother Church and every one of its branches.

Her whole concept was oneness, uniting mankind in universal brotherhood. And the goal? The final conquest of sin through the ever-operative, regenerative, healing Christ, Truth. The prophet Habakkuk foresaw this day. He says, "The earth shall be filled with the knowledge of the glory of the Lord, as the waters cover the sea" (Hab. 2:14).

The question arises, How may we help this great Cause? What should be our daily prayer and metaphysical work for our vision of Church? What is it that puts us to sleep and would make us forget and neglect our duty? Isn't it animal magnetism, the name Mrs. Eddy assigns to all evil?

We don't work metaphysically for Church, the divine idea. This wonderful "structure of Truth and Love" doesn't need our work any more than man, the image and likeness of God, does. But *we* need to work to keep our vision of Church so clear that in the human and divine coincidence, where the human is hourly yielding to the divine, we may prove that the institution, or organization, is fulfilling its mission. Seen as the human appearing of Church, of the spiritual structure, the Church of Christ, Scientist, is the most powerful, most vital, most impregnable institution in the world. It is indeed a living power. It never hurts but blesses all mankind.

What can heal crime, destroy poverty, sensuality, greed, lust, dishonesty, hate, but the power of the Christ—revealing Church, "the structure of Truth and Love; whatever rests upon and proceeds from divine Principle"? Corruption in government, rivalry among nations, clashing of races, famine, pestilence, poverty, overpopulation—for these, human methods hold no adequate answer. But Christian Science does. Mrs. Eddy saw this, and she left the Church of Christ, Scientist, for us to prove it.

We have seen that animal magnetism is the enemy that must be overcome. And how does animal magnetism claim to work? Its action is malpractice, wrong practice based on the belief that there is life, substance, and intelligence in matter, that man is mortal, that there are many minds, and that evil is power. The tool of animal magnetism is aggressive mental suggestion. Mrs. Eddy says it is our duty to defend ourselves daily against this evil (see *Manual of The Mother Church*, Art. VIII, Sect. 6). How do we do this? Through a love so pure that it enables us to claim our spiritual identity in the likeness of the Father.

Aggressive mental suggestion comes under the guise of our own thought. What makes us feel, I don't love church; I resent the organization and those who are working there; I'll withdraw my name in the church election; I'm going to withdraw my membership; I can't or don't want to give to church financially or metaphysically; and so on and on? And especially, I can't heal; I don't want to go into the practice of Christian Science?

What is it that tempts us to believe and rehearse error concerning the movement, the membership, the services? Our church services heal when we put enough love in them. The healing power of the Christ cannot be stopped. Through growing spiritualization of thought each member should earnestly strive to unite daily with the spiritual concept of Church. Let us start our daily mental work for church, for ourselves, for the world, with an ever-deepening love for God, a broadening understanding of His allness and of our ability to demonstrate this, and with a growing gratitude for Christian Science and its Discoverer and Founder.

From this basis let us reject, deny, and trample on every aggressive suggestion of personal sense that would mesmerize us into sleep and apathy. Error is never our own thought. It is never a condition, situation, or person, but simply a false suggestion, a mesmeric lie, *nothingness*.

Then we really will have what Paul so delightfully expresses as a church without a wrinkle. He says in his Epistle to the Ephesians, "Christ ... loved the church, and gave himself for it; that he might sanctify and cleanse it ..., that he might present it to himself a glorious church, not having spot, or wrinkle, or any such thing; but that it should be holy and without blemish" (5:25–27). Let us see that the Church we love, the Church we individually include, is without a wrinkle!

Mrs. Eddy saw the great importance of Church in human experience. Hence her words, "The Church, more than any other institution, at present is the cement of society, and it should be the bulwark of civil and religious liberty" (*Miscellaneous Writings*, pp. 144–145).

—*L. Ivimy Gwalter*

THE CHURCH MANUAL

Christian Scientists have for their instruction the Scriptures, the writings of Mrs. Eddy, which open to them the Scriptures, and the *Church Manual*, the rules of which help them to apply what they have been taught. The Bible, understood through Christian Science, is aiding its students individually to live in Christian discipleship; the *Manual* of The Church of Christ, Scientist, in providing that Christian Scientists shall work together, is helping them collectively to live in Christian fellowship. The teaching of the Scriptures and the Christian Science text-book bring about the individual correction of thought, while the rules of the *Church Manual* make possible right action through groups of individuals and through the whole body of Scientists. So, the Bible, *Science and Health*, and the *Manual* are equally important in their places. The *Manual* bears definite relation to the other two books in that it shows us how to take the steps that will bring their teaching into our lives in all necessary relations with our fellow-men. It safeguards and regenerates Christian fellowship by promoting the best possible form of church organization. For these reasons, therefore, it can no more be dispensed with than can the Scriptures or the Christian Science text-book.

Of the Bible Mrs. Eddy has written: "Christian Scientists are fishers of men. The Bible is our sea-beaten Rock. It guides the fishermen. It stands the storm. It engages the attention and enriches the being of all men" (*Christian Science Sentinel*, March 31, 1906). Christian Scientists themselves know what place the Christian Science text-book holds in their regeneration; how it makes plain the words of prophet, apostle, and of the Master himself; how it brings Christian healing into human experience today. And concerning the *Manual* Mrs. Eddy has said: "Of this I am sure, that each rule and by-law in the Manual will increase the spirituality of him who obeys it, invigorate his capacity to heal the sick, to comfort such as mourn, and to awaken the sinner" (*Sentinel*, Sept. 12, 1903). In keeping with the law and order set forth in the *Manual*, we have the Sunday Lesson-Sermons, the mid-week testimony meetings, the provision of monthly, weekly, and daily reading-matter, the board of lecturers, the Christian Science reading-rooms, the publication committee work, the rotation of church officers, etc., while, in keeping with its instructions, students

are being taught and patients are being healed in all the world. Great reforms, indeed, are going on through the united action for good which operates through the Christian Science movement, and the outward and visible activities bear witness to the inward and spiritual understanding, which is itself being quickened by the law and order and discipline of right organization.

It is best for the Christian Scientist at present that he is not allowed to live to himself. His place in organization teaches him many things that he cannot learn otherwise, for it lifts him from the selfish consideration of his personal problems to the unselfish support of an impersonal cause. Within the ample boundaries of the Christian Science organization he finds multiplied opportunities for surrendering his own will, his own opinion, and his own comfort to the good of the whole,— opportunities unafforded even by the home or by any outside life in the world; and he is cheered by good example and by happy fellowship to higher faith in good as the ends of organization are worked out together.

If, then, the *Church Manual*, with the organization for which it provides, has so large a place in the establishment and growth of Christian Science, it is essential that Christian Scientists be keenly alive to its provisions and its demands. Continual fidelity, for instance, to the instruction found in Article VIII., Section 1, that "neither animosity nor mere personal attachment" shall govern motives and actions; to the warning in the same paragraph against "prophesying, judging, condemning, counseling, influencing or being influenced erroneously;" to the demand for a charitable attitude toward all religious, medical, and legal points of view; to the adoption, so insistently urged, of the spirit of the golden rule,—this fidelity, we know, will help in the making over of human nature, until in some fair day by-laws to provide for such consistent Christian behavior shall be no longer necessary. And it is unquestionably true that he who really does heed the requirement set forth in the *Manual* concerning Jesus' teaching that each shall go to his brother alone and tell him of his fault before publishing it to others, accepts a discipline which makes him in deed as well as in profession a genuine Christian Scientist.

Because the question of church organization is so vital a matter, it becomes naturally an important point to protect. A Christian Scientist who cannot at the moment be made suddenly disloyal to the Bible, to the Christian Science text-book or to its writer, can perhaps, through innumerable arguments, be persuaded into a lukewarm attitude toward church organization. Indifference, restlessness, criticism that is mere fault-finding and is not constructively helpful, are the symptoms of coming under such persuasion. To prevent this each member needs to keep his thoughts warm and loving toward all church activities; to be cheerfully in his place at meetings whenever possible; to be helpfully interested in every detail of cooperative work, though this does not mean necessarily that he shall take part, personally, in every church undertaking; for the quietest and least conspicuous church-member is sometimes best serving the church. It does mean, however, that we must guard zealously our love for organization, even in its present incomplete form, that we may not hinder its growth into greater beauty and utility.

Indifference to organization indicates that we believe we value the Scriptures and the Christian Science text-book, but refuse the discipline their teaching asks of us through the rules and by-laws of the *Manual*. Finding and keeping a place within organization means sometimes the surrender of ease and self-will, but it means, too, shelter and safety and the right to peace. So long, then, as the Leader of the Christian Science movement sees there is need for organization to establish Christian Science, no student may fancy that he has rightly "outgrown" organization. The Christian Scientist is a standard-bearer within The Church of Christ, Scientist, and he who remains loyally and lovingly at his post best serves God, all humanity, and himself.

It may be said, truly, that the inspiration for the *Church Manual* is found in the life of Mrs. Eddy. Everything asked of Christian Scientists in maintaining the cause beyond and above all personal interests, Mrs. Eddy herself has done before them. Had she consulted only her own comfort she might have been tempted to apply what she knows of God just to the working out of her own salvation. Instead, she has labored forty years and more to give of her store to the world; she has been impelled to found the church with all its educational branches, and to protect its growing activities; she has foregone ease, and has bound herself to this task, that we, too, may find the Christ-healing for our sin and pain. Consistent and blessed is the Christian Scientist who can bind himself with her until many more shall find their healing and until The Church of Christ, Scientist, shall stand in good will to all men, radiant and triumphant in the earth.

—Blanche Hersey Hogue

THE CONSISTENCY THAT IS IN CHRIST

*T*he writer who said, "Consistency is a paste jewel that only cheap men cherish," turned a neat counterphrase on a well-known saying, but he did so at the expense of a truism, a truism which has been expressed endlessly, but never more powerfully than in Paul's "Jesus Christ the same yesterday, and today, and for ever" (Heb. 13:8). This word *consistency* may seem to have contradictory connotations, but in its truly scientific sense it means being right and going ahead accordingly. Happily the Christian Scientist can know too much to waste time and effort on what Ralph Waldo Emerson called "a foolish consistency." As a disciple of the Master he can increasingly shape his demonstration of Christ into that sameness, that undeviating practice of the truth he proclaims.

This spiritual radicalism became to Isaiah a voice behind him saying (30:21), "This is the way, walk ye in it, when ye turn to the right hand, and when ye turn to the left." Immutability is a quality properly attributable to God, but the deific changelessness is not a static condition. The undeviating goodness of God as expressed in His works, man including the universe, must also be an infinite variation, and endless newness which testifies not to fixity, but to the ceaseless motion of Mind. The returning spring means not only revival but origination. Divine origination is the crying need of individuals and movements. Consistently growth comes not out of death, but out of the spontaneity of Life, God.

The great inconsistency of the ages has been the attributing of the finite to the infinite. Brahmanism holds that the world of matter is unreal, illusion, yet that Brahma or Deity made it; hence that the only escape from the illusory external world is absorption in Deity. Such impersonalization would inevitably bring about obliteration, and such impersonality, if attainable, would be oblivion.

Inconsistencies, as in Brahmanism, have in all ages plagued man-made religions and philosophies. To conceive of a universe in which both good and evil exist is to make God the author of evil, Truth the producer of error. Zoroaster set forth a dualism of a good spirit, or God, and an evil spirit, or devil, both accepted as real, but in constant conflict, an inconsistent teaching, inasmuch as it advanced the proposition that one phase of reality can destroy another. Only in Christian Science do we find a sure ground of consistency, a ground whereon the reality, existence of good, repudiates error by preclusion of it. Only in Christian Science can one consistently deal with the finite as a falsity, not a fact.

On page 583 of the Christian Science text-book, *Science and Health with Key to the Scriptures*, Mary Baker Eddy defines *Christ* as "the divine manifestation of God, which comes to the flesh to destroy incarnate error." This definition is consistent with the lines in the Preface to that same book, where she describes the healing works of Christian Science in these words (p. xi): "They are the sign of Immanuel, or 'God with us,'—a divine influence ever present in human consciousness and repeating itself, coming now as was promised aforetime,

To preach deliverance to the captives [of sense],
And recovering of sight to the blind,
To set at liberty them that are bruised."

Consistent also are references in *Science and Health* to Christ as the spiritual idea, the spiritual idea of sonship, the indestructible man, immortal manhood, the true idea of God, the offspring of Spirit, and many others.

In *Rudimental Divine Science* Mrs. Eddy says (p. 7), "The infinite and subtler conceptions and consistencies of Christian Science are set forth in my work Science and Health." These more subtle conceptions and consistencies are not grasped by casual or sporadic reading of the textbook or by mere excerpts pried from their context. Rather are they arrived at only by relating and reconciling all statements to the basic truths of Christian Science, and by conscious effort to know and manifest more of the divine nature, the unity of God and man, one's true being and selfhood. The subtler conceptions thus grasped dispel seeming ambiguities and inconsistencies and maintain the unfailing consistencies of the text with true conceptions of its meanings.

To grasp these subtler conceptions and consistencies one must seek always to measure all amplification, both in *Science and Health* and in our Leader's other writings, to the foundational facts of divine Science. These facts stem from the basic allness and oneness of God and man; the unity, yet the distinctness, of cause and effect, Mind and man, Principle and idea. *Science and Health* repeats again and again the necessity to resolve all existence into the unity and distinctness of noumenon and phenomena, God and His thoughts.

The simplicity that is in Christian Science, then, is in the truth that whatever exists must be in the category of either God or man, Principle or its idea. The correct understanding of the terminology of Christian Science is determined by the facts of being, not by words. When Christ Jesus said (John 14:6), "No man cometh unto the Father, but by me," he showed plainly that in the unity of being, God is primary and man is the derivative, and that to know man, one's real self, is to know God, the Father, whose reflection is man, the son.

The author of *Science and Health* wrote for all states and stages of human consciousness. So even the more casual and superficial reading of her writings will inevitably meet for every reader the requirements and possibilities of the moment. The most obvious meanings are both preventive and curative of error. The further the study and practice, and study and practice cannot rightly be divorced, the more subtle are the meanings, yet the more crystal clear and simple. The deeper things of God and man are contained in *Science and Health* and are accessible and available. The deeper the spiritual waters of Truth, the more limpid they become. And in those depths is easiest and safest navigation. There is no danger in the subtler conceptions and consistencies.

A certain author prefaces his book with the statement that of all words he most dislikes *consistency*. But surely that must have been because he had not drunk deep enough of the inspiration which reveals the deep things of Principle and the simplicity and consistency that are in Christ. A foolish consistency is the slave of precedent. Not so was Christ Jesus, who followed precedent only when it was based on Principle and under highest right. He had little respect for the traditions of the elders, which too often perverted judgment.

Christ Jesus never deviated from strictest ethical standards of thought and conduct based on Principle. He looked for no relief from matter, material remedies or methods, or from mortal mind. He stood always for spiritual radicalism and for conduct consistent therewith. His course in all contingencies was never appeasement or compromise with error, but an intelligent, balanced progressivism, in which he held himself to what our Leader has described as radical reliance on Truth. His demonstration of Christ was complete, and he is our example.

On the cross Jesus knew that to prove the supremacy of Christ over pain and injury, and even death, was far more important to him and to humanity than was any temporary easement he might have had by drinking the pain reliever offered him by his executioners. He knew that yielding to material means and methods invariably is at the expense of spiritual understanding and growth. Jesus drank the cup necessary to demonstration, but not the stupefying cup of appeasement or concession. As followers of Christ Jesus, shall we not strive for the same sense of spiritual values he displayed at all times, and shall we not glory in the simplicity, the humility, and the consistency that are in Christ?

If we follow Christ consistently, we shall find that we can demonstrate Christ as surely as Jesus did, and ultimately as completely. We shall find that in proportion to our consistent adherence to the ethical and spiritual standard set up and held up by our Master, we also shall prove that, in the words of Jesus (John 3:34), "God giveth not the Spirit by measure unto [us]."

—John M. Tutt

CROWNING THE CROSS

⁓

*I*n studying the familiar and well-loved emblem of Christian Science, the cross and crown, which must ever be the hallmark of authentic Christian Science literature, one is impressed with the character of the crown. He discovers it to be the opposite of the crown of thorns; rather is it a crown of power and authority, of triumph and rejoicing. May not the cross symbolize the way of material sense, the human way of dream and suffering, and the crown the way of Truth, of Love's reality? We need to keep clearly in thought that the crown is not material. It is the crown of Spirit, signifying spiritual understanding and rejoicing. As we follow the way of the crown, the cross disappears, is eliminated from consciousness.

On page 350 of *Miscellaneous Writings* Mary Baker Eddy says, "I issue no arguments, and cause none to be used in mental practice, which consign people to suffering." The way of the cross, then, is not the way of Love, of divine Principle. It is the way of material dream; and this waking dream, like the sleeping dream, has no self, no ego, through which it can be identified. It is always a dream calling itself a dreamer. However, it does at times seem to mesmerize one into claiming it and giving it a selfhood, carrying the cross of suffering, of belief in separation from the good which is God. Through the crown of spiritual understanding, however, one finds his true selfhood in Spirit, and the cross fades into nothingness. How beautifully one finds this fading out of the cross illustrated in our Leader's poem *Christ and Christmas*.

In one of her best-loved poems Mrs. Eddy writes (*Poems*, p. 12):

"I kiss the cross, and wake to know
A world more bright."

What does it mean to "kiss the cross"? May it not mean that we are to see in the error which the cross represents a challenge to our understanding of the truth of being as the constant and uninterrupted expression of divine Mind; an opportunity to demonstrate the presence and power of divine Love and to be its unmarred reflection? Is not this what Jesus meant when he bade his followers take up the cross and follow him? In order to do this one must be fully convinced of the truth he declares and its omnipotence, its infallible law. He must intelligently and unflinchingly trust that law and its ceaseless activity, operating unhindered by false, material concepts.

A woman carrying in belief a cross of physical discord said to the practitioner to whom she had turned for help, "Of course, I want to be healed physically, but not before I have learned every lesson this experience has to teach me." This willingness to kiss the cross, to learn the lessons of Truth, necessarily brought a quick mental and physical healing. Was not this the mental attitude of Jacob when he wrestled with the angel and said, "I will not let thee go, except thou bless me"(Gen. 32:26)?

In thus learning to kiss the cross, one ceases to fear it, to resent it, or to complain about it. Rather does he set about diligently and triumphantly to learn the truth of its superlative opposite. He learns that the cross is never a material or physical difficulty, demanding a material or physical remedy, but rather a mental perversion, to be corrected mentally. He learns the marvels of divine Science, the glowing truths of real being. He learns to displace every ungodlike trait of character with the Christ-qualities of divine Mind.

Such a one learns to love rather than to hate or fear, to be grateful rather than resentful, to put off the falsities of criticism, condemnation, impatience, self-will, discouragement. Discouragement has been defined by someone as "disappointed self-will." So one learns to put off self-will, whether it appears as a good self-will or the contrary. He learns to wait on God's *good* will, which is always operating in his behalf. He learns to displace intellectual wrestlings with scientific humility, to wear the crown of unity rather than bear the cross of separation. To kiss the cross with understanding is to crown the cross with demonstration and "wake to know a world more bright."

We must learn to put a crown on every cross, wherever it may appear, and however high we may have to climb to do so. It may be a cross representing false theology, mistaken teaching about God and man, presenting an inconsistent God, who knows and permits both good and evil, and man subject to these conflicting powers, a God consisting of both Spirit and matter and so continually divided against Himself. Here is an opportunity, indeed, to place upon this cross, wherever it may be, the shining crown of the teaching of Christ Jesus that God is one

God and eternally good: a God of life who knows not death, a God who knows not fear or hate, but a God of love who omnipotently decrees love for His creation. Let us consecratedly work, then, to crown every cross of ignorance, bigotry, intolerance, and ecclesiastical despotism with the radiant diadem of spiritual understanding, omnipotent Truth.

Does our neighbor appear to be carrying a cross? Let us hasten to crown it with reflected Love, keeping our own consciousness undarkened by cross-forming shadows. This Love-lit crown will assuredly help him on his way. While we may not without his request presume to give him specific treatment, it is our privilege, nay, our sacred duty, in our own thinking to put upon that cross the crown of rejoicing, the understanding of its unreality. We are privileged to know the universal love of the Father, who afflicteth not His children, but ever holds them in the light and law of Love and harmony. We are privileged to know that nothing exists that can resist or that is resisting this divine law of Love. Then we can with joy and peace leave our neighbor under that law of Love, aware that it will unfold to him the truth of his being and the unreality of the cross he seems to bear. At the same time we fail not to extend to him the kindly human touch which reveals that Love reflected in love. Is not this fulfilling the command, "Thou shalt love thy neighbour as thyself"?

No matter, then, how heavy may seem the cross or how long it seems to have been borne, one must keep in sight the diadem which is crowning each step of the way with clearer, fresher views of reality. Through this revealing spiritual understanding, one finds the crown of power and dominion and rejoices in his true being as the reflected glory of God's pure spiritual being, eternally free from the weight of either cross or crown material.

—*Margaret Morrison*

FIDELITY

❧

The peace of the world rests wholly upon the devotion of thought to imperishable good. Because reality alone can be eternal, it is upon the thinking of those who perceive Mind, God, to be All-in-all that the security and progress of mankind depend. Such thinking inevitably partakes of the perfect nature of that which is perceived and is evidenced in what appear to be human affairs in the degree of its fidelity to Truth.

A dictionary defines *fidelity* as "strict adherence to truth or fact." The fact that consciousness is fundamental, a pronouncement acknowledged by noted physicists, though not understood by them in its spiritual significance and depth, has been clearly elucidated in the writings of Mary Baker Eddy, who deduces her conclusions from the demonstrable knowledge that God is the only Mind. In so doing, Mrs. Eddy has set forth as fully and exactly as can be done by means of human language the irrefutable consequence of this divine fact, which is the unreality of matter. She has presented this fact in the only way a divine fact can be correctly regarded—as indivisible truth, to be accepted in its entirety or not at all.

The inspired guidance of her presentation of Truth appeared in the full measure of her own acceptance of and adherence to the truth revealed. A summation of the teaching of Christian Science is given by her on page 468 of the textbook, *Science and Health with Key to the Scriptures*, in "the scientific statement of being." It is in part: "There is no life, truth, intelligence, nor substance in matter. All is infinite Mind and its infinite manifestation, for God is All-in-all." This profound and ultimate statement of Truth was born of our Leader's fidelity to what she spiritually discerned.

From the time she turned to the Bible for solace from what appeared to be a fatal injury and comprehended the nature of Jesus' healing of the palsied man, there was fealty to the truth which she progressively perceived. Her unswerving conviction that everything real is good and divinely mental continued and grew in the face of insistent claims of error. The steadfastness with which she maintained as individual consciousness her unfolding spiritual outlook made possible the progressive appearing of Truth, understood and demonstrated. In her autobiography, *Retrospection and Introspection*, we read (pp. 28–29), "This is my endeavor, to be a Christian, to assimilate the character and practice of the anointed; and no motive can cause a surrender of this effort."

The ability to demonstrate Christian Science demands unvarying adherence to divine Mind. It requires that true identity be accepted as one's conscious knowing. It means the steadfast demonstration of divine Mind, which includes the truths unknown to mortal mind. Christian Science teaches that a first glimpse of true being is not an apprehension of something external, but it is a disclosing, or unfoldment, of that which is innate, an appearing of the immortal nature of all real being or existence. Therefore logic compels recognition that the truths which are discerned by those receptive to the understanding that divine Mind is All-in-all must be continuously realized and maintained in order that this receptive thought may approximate and demonstrate progressively the all-inclusive activity of pure intelligence, Love.

As we consider the words of our Leader just quoted, we see that to assimilate, to become similar to, the character or the individuality of the anointed, is a divinely mental experience which cannot be dissociated from the habitual spiritual standpoint of our thought. It was Peter's unswerving spiritual point of view which raised Dorcas, a woman "full of good works and almsdeeds," from the dead. The account of this healing in the ninth chapter of the book of Acts indicates that Peter put out of the room all negative thought and then lifted her up and presented her alive.

Individuals reflect the indestructible nature of the Love that is Life only to the degree that they know Mind's creation as Mind knows it to be and remain unmoved by the presentations of finite sense. The Master's understanding of the truth of being made it possible for him instantaneously to heal the sick and feed thousands. His fidelity to Mind and Mind's creation constituted his character, was evidenced in his practice, and proved Life to be eternal.

Christ Jesus gave to mankind the outstanding proof of faithful adherence to the reality of being. He remained unmoved by the manifold phases which evil assumed to discredit and discourage him and abode confidently and courageously in the assurance of man's present and forever perfection. Throughout his ministry there is undeniable evidence of the unfolding dominion available in the hourly experience of everyone who will wholeheartedly discipline thought to maintain the viewpoint of the great Way-shower. Mrs. Eddy writes of his teaching on the hillside near the Galilean sea as follows (*Retrospection and Introspection*, p. 91): "In this simplicity, and with such fidelity, we see Jesus ministering to the spiritual needs of all who placed themselves under his care, always leading them into the divine order, under the sway of his own perfect understanding."

The undeviating spiritual standpoint of Jesus' thought is shown in his statement (John 14:10), "The words that I speak unto you I speak not of myself: but the Father that dwelleth in me, he doeth the works." The continuance of this saying indicates that he claimed for himself no power which could not be fully understood and utilized by all: "He that believeth on me, the works that I do shall he do also; and greater works than these shall he do; because I go unto my Father." Through his vital, abiding sense of reality Jesus demonstrated his true identity, expressed in his words (John 10:30), "I and my Father are one." Had his followers perceived and practiced the complete integrity of his example, no dark ages would have obscured the light of Life's revelation.

The proof given in Biblical record and by the Christian Science movement that the demonstration of God's omnipotence belongs to no special age, time, or individual, establishes as invariable the nature of that which is infinite. Then it is understandable that thought which accepts Truth merely as theory and in the name of Christian Science, and consequently turns to it only upon occasion for a remedy, does not partake of Truth's changeless nature. Far more than being an admirable quality of disposition or character, fidelity is a quality of thought essential to the progressive appearing of the love of God.

Invariableness of spiritual outlook has distinguished those past and present thinkers who have perceived something of God's allness. Abraham, whom Mrs. Eddy defines as fidelity, had devotion of thought equal to leaving all familiar landmarks, thereby establishing not only enduring health and great prosperity for himself, but a more spiritual concept of Deity for a nation. Now, as then, willingness to relinquish old false landmarks and mental habits for fidelity to one's spiritual sense of being evidences the presence of ever-unfolding spiritual peace and freedom.

Man's continuing conscious knowing of the divine fact constitutes fidelity. Since reality has neither beginning nor ending, the continuity of being is indisputably the truth of being. Continuity, therefore, is the essence of immortal Principle, God, and must characterize the standpoint of any thinker who would demonstrate this ever-operative Principle. There can be no self-indulgent or unalert acceptance of mortality for ourselves or anyone else if we would have reality—the eternal Mind, which constitutes its own divine appearing—progressively present, determining our character and practice.

This devotion of thought to whatever one already apprehends of real being alone can fulfill "the first and great commandment" as given by the Master (Matt. 22:37), "Thou shalt love the Lord thy God with all thy heart, and with all thy soul, and with all thy mind." The perception of the allness of God is a revealing or unfoldment in individual consciousness of inherent Truth, and it also requires one's entire allegiance.

Proportionably as pure affection is permitted to permeate our standpoint of being, imperishable Love is seen as embracing humanity in its own eternal peace and perfection. The timeless words of Paul in the epistle to the Romans were a plea for fidelity (12:9): "Let love be without dissimulation."

—Ellen Watt

FREEDOM FROM SUFFERING

*F*reedom, complete freedom, is man's precious heritage as the son of God, not only freedom from evil, but freedom to be the perfect man whom God makes in His likeness. Man's spiritual perfection includes freedom from mental and bodily suffering as surely as from social and civil bondage.

The whole human family seeks respite from suffering. No one wants it, but everyone at some time, in some measure, is faced with it. Suffering sense asks: "What is suffering? Whence comes it? Why must I suffer?"

To these questions, literally thousands have found the answer in the teachings and practice of Christian Science. Not only has this Science exposed the fatuous nature and origin of pain and suffering, but more important, it has revealed the true and lasting spiritual remedy for them by making plain to mankind the truth concerning God and man in His image. "If we are Christians on all moral questions," writes Mary Baker Eddy in *Science and Health with Key to the Scriptures* (p. 373), "but are in darkness as to the physical exemption which Christianity includes, then we must have more faith in God on this subject and be more alive to His promises."

The Bible contains many sharp illustrations of the irreconcilability of opposites: A fountain does not send forth at the same place sweet water and bitter; a fruit tree cannot produce both figs and olives. That suffering and harmony fall into the classification of opposites does not occur to many people. Yet, suffering and harmony are contrary to each other. They neither mix nor mingle. One is true; the other is false.

The basis of this logic is the fact that, as Christian Science teaches, God is infinite good without an opposite or equal. God, infinite Spirit, being all-inclusive, all-pervasive, all substance, neither produces, permits, nor blends with an opposite. Evil, then, must be supposititious.

Since good is all—the only reality—evil, though seeming to be actual, cannot in truth exist in the allness of its opposite, infinite Spirit, God.

Carrying this reasoning to its logical conclusion, Mrs. Eddy writes (*ibid.*, p. 186), "If pain is as real as the absence of pain, both must be immortal; and if so, harmony cannot be the law of being."

Here Mrs. Eddy clearly draws the issue: Which is true, harmony or suffering? And, in her usual directness, she leaves no doubt that not only is pain false, but harmony is the law of God. Just think of the implications of this statement! When understood, what can it not do to annihilate one of mankind's most feared, most time-honored, and most troublesome foes!

From a material standpoint, the origin and nature of human pain and suffering are conjectural. Material methods of treatment consistently regard suffering as a reality. Centuries of false education and fear have evolved the erroneous concept of man as mortal and as subject to pain and suffering, of mind as being in matter, and of sense as being material. Vast sums of money and thousands of hours have been devoted to alleviating human misery through material research and material medicine. Yet, human suffering still challenges men and baffles them.

Because suffering is a nonentity, a nonactuality, in the real and divine sense, it does not exist where material investigation looks for it, and it does not have the substance which material sense ascribes to it. It is an illusion, the product of mortal belief, and can be understood only as such. So the search for it as something—a reality—is vain, hopeless. Of this vital point Mrs. Eddy says (*ibid.*, p. 86), "Mortal mind sees what it believes as certainly as it believes what it sees."

Almost everybody acknowledges that a dream has no entity; that is, it does not possess substance, intelligence, law, or reality. In physical therapeutics, so-called mental ills are readily classified as delusion and thus are relegated to their proper category of unreality. More and more, as all human ills, both physical and mental, are seen to consist solely of the stuff that dreams are made of will they be correctly classified and successfully treated through spiritual therapy alone.

Christian Science is practicing and demonstrating today that all human ills, with the sense of pain and suffering which accompanies them, are truly healed only as they are seen to have no origin in reality—God and His perfect creation.

The life and teachings of Christ Jesus stir the human heart to grapple with pain and suffering, the foes of human progress, on the basis of spiritual logic, reason, and demonstration. Jesus said (John 14:6), "I am the way, the truth, and the life." And he proved his words by his deeds, healing the sick, raising the dead, and comforting the sorrowing.

The master Christian demonstrated God's power over every phase of human suffering and indicated to his followers that they could and should do likewise. During his three days in the tomb, Christ Jesus illustrated, without the aid of any material remedies, the availability and adequacy of spiritual power to meet and master pain and suffering of the most severe and serious nature. Through the understanding of God and His harmonious government of man, many today are proving that pain and suffering are readily subject to the power and love of God.

The answer to all suffering is to understand the actuality, the naturalness and normalcy of good as God's law governing all reality. At no point can man as God's reflection receive, include, possess, or express a condition or a quality the opposite of his origin, divine Love.

Because God knows no disease, pain, sorrow, or suffering, man, God's image, is incapable of experiencing such ills. Human generation, growth, time, space, death, the so-called hereafter, cannot alter this spiritual fact of being.

Man has never been sick, diseased, in pain, nor has he died and been transmuted by some mysterious process into a state of perfection, nor will he ever be. Actually, man, the man of God's making, is forever in a state of perfect being and can never get out of it.

The acknowledgment of this spiritual fact acts upon the human consciousness as an irresistible, unfailing law of healing. It dispels fear, ushers in trust in God's allness, removes doubt, and establishes calm and tranquillity.

God's law of harmony acts upon human consciousness to nullify educated expectancy of pain under given conditions, breaks the mesmerism of dread, and enables the individual, with calm and poised certainty, to stand staunchly for the demonstration of spiritual dominion over the lie of pain and suffering.

Unafraid, spiritually illumined thought looks right through the ghost of suffering straight into the present fact of man's freedom and harmony. Inspiration stands unmoved by mortal mind's shouts of danger, neglect, carelessness, and rests firmly on the foundation of demonstrable, spiritual understanding.

A student of Christian Science experienced just how practical and dependable is the healing, saving power of divine Love at a time when pain and suffering seemed humanly unbearable. He learned that there is no such thing as unbearable pain or pain of any description, because for every degree of the belief of pain, there is a greater measure of God's love.

For several weeks he could find no ease or comfort in any physical position. Sleepless nights and days dragged on and on. He had sought the help of a Christian Science practitioner, whose steadfast and comforting metaphysical aid he clearly felt as he himself strove to lift his own thought above the sense of suffering into a clearer realization of the presence of good alone.

Finally, one night after several weeks of suffering, he decided he would get out of bed, cease trying to find comfort in matter or a comfortable spot to lay the body, and sit straight up in a chair and just work firmly and continuously, no matter how long this took, to establish in his consciousness the fact that harmony exists in spiritual sense alone—the sense of being conferred by Soul, God. At first, it seemed impossible to remain still and quiet. The student, however, was soon able to take control of his thinking, then of his body. He was then able to sit perfectly still and calm.

Vigorously, clearly, firmly he denied the testimony of material sense and affirmed the presence, power, and unfailing action of the law of Love. He realized that since God, Soul, was his life, he could have no sense or feeling of himself or his condition underived from Soul; that right there, every moment, even while material sense said nothing could be felt but pain, actually nothing was going on but the consciousness of health, harmony, power, and freedom. This line of work was carried on for about three hours without interruption.

At length, the student's thought became so clear in the truth and so strong in the conviction of what he was knowing, that nothing was left in his consciousness to which the sense of pain could attach itself. He could almost feel the dream of pain fade and the influx of harmony take charge of him mentally and bodily. Presently he was completely free; he arose, went back to bed, and slept soundly the rest of the night. That was the end of the trouble.

Christian Science demonstrates painless being to be the present fact, attainable here and now. In Revelation we read (21:1–4): "And I saw a new heaven and a new earth: for the first heaven and the first earth were passed away; and there was no more sea. . . . And I heard a great voice out of heaven saying, Behold, the tabernacle of God is with men. . . . And God shall wipe away all tears from their eyes; and there shall be no more death, neither sorrow, nor crying, neither shall there be any more pain: for the former things are passed away."

—Inman H. Douglass

"FROM ZONE TO ZONE"

*G*od's universe is one infinite, spiritual reflection of divine substance and Life. Throughout the length, breadth, depth, and height of the universe the laws of harmony continuously operate. Divine Science is the government of this measureless realm filled with divine ideas and their identities obedient to their creative Mind. Here are spiritually scientific statements which hold vast import for students of world affairs.

Spiritual facts, when discerned and accepted, affect global events as naturally as individual situations. As humanity progresses out of the chaos of materialistic belief, inspired thought, becoming aware of the unaltered divine order, necessarily eagerly reaches out for further spiritual perception wherewith to behold the unshaken reality of things.

Spiritual perception alone cognizes the eternal unity of universal existence and the control of divine Science. Through such penetration, everlasting Love, impartial, constant, ever Godward in its impulsions, is seen to be the only animating power of all elements and formations, of all intelligence and action. Wholly and continually the universe of Mind's ideas reflects divine, scientific order, functioning in accord with supreme harmony.

Necessarily that which emanates from God must exist within the infinitude of divine Mind, partake of the nature of Soul, and be formed of the substance of Love, for the terms Mind, Soul, Love, God, are synonymous in Science. The universe contains only celestial bodies held in the unbroken rhythm of heavenly concord, controlled by the moral and spiritual forces of Mind, and dwelling in the atmosphere of Soul. The seasons of the universe are periods of constant spiritual unfoldment which bring forth fadeless evidence of the presence of divine qualities throughout creation.

God eternally coexists with His universe, with that which is embraced in His all-inclusiveness. Speaking of Christian Science, Mary Baker Eddy writes (*Miscellaneous Writings*, p. 364): "It is not a search after wisdom, it *is* wisdom: it is God's right hand grasping the universe,—all time, space, immortality, thought, extension, cause, and effect; constituting and governing all identity, individuality, law, and power." This holy provision ensures constant perfection, endless government, and changeless sovereignty for universal existence.

At no time and in no part of the universe can there occur a break in the divine control. God cannot be excluded for an instant from infinitude, and His laws are established for eternity. Preservation permeates their every action of unfoldment. Without opposition, resistance, or delay, the majesty of spiritual law pursues its glorious way. Thus universal manifestation, rising from boundless perfection, lives, moves, and has being in terms of foreverness, allness, divinity.

Knowing only the existence of immortality in the substance of Spirit, untouched by sin and death, the universe expresses the glory of God, radiant, eternal reality. All identities which comprise the universe exist in unity because, in the divine order, each idea is tributary directly to divine Mind, always sharing its inexhaustible essence. Thus the grandeur of all existence, indestructible throughout its vastness, is maintained by God's Science.

In contrast with this unified immensity and stability of everlasting perfection, belief in a power apart from God is like a grain of sand on a tidal shore. Human, erring sense, having no conception of infinity or perfection, believes that the universe is material and divided into both discordant and harmonious parts. It believes in subdivisions of the earth named zones, then in belief attributes to these zones certain conditions of good or evil. The frigid zones are believed to be regions of the universe where storms originate which spread disaster. The torrid zone is believed to be an expanse where fevers and pestilences breed. Other divisions are labeled earthquake zones, hurricane zones, and so on.

When humanity becomes involved in the acceptance of evil belief, the subdivisions of erroneous sense multiply and there seem to be enemy zones whence springs the anguish of war, battle zones where carnage stains the earth, and danger zones where destruction awaits the traveler. Mortal mind defines these zones as areas where evil holds sway and from which good has been eliminated. Then mortal belief declares that if men dwell within, or pass through, such territory, they are subject to disaster and destruction. Having no concept of God's infinite kingdom, mortal sense would like to believe in these little spaces where it might reign for a season.

But God's Science grasps all time and space, all cause and effect, all power and law. There can be no such thing as territory where evil holds control, where God's law has ceased to function. There is no space deserted by God, or forbidden to God. There is no opportunity for error to start, accumulate, or dominate. The assumption that there is a moment when God is not supreme is mortal illusion.

David knew the falsity of error's claim to possess and govern a zone of existence anywhere. In declaring the boundless presence of God, good, he wrote: "Whither shall I go from thy spirit? or whither shall I flee from thy presence? If I ascend up into heaven, thou art there: if I make my bed in hell, behold, thou art there. If I take the wings of the morning, and dwell in the uttermost parts of the sea; even there shall thy hand lead me, and thy right hand shall hold me" (Ps. 139: 7–10).

God's omnipotence precludes the possibility of a danger zone in creation. Man never passes through evil's realm, or exists for a moment within it, for evil, being nonexistent, possesses no domain. All ideas of the creator live and disport themselves in perfect safety throughout the endless realm of Mind. They know no fear, no peril, in boundless Love. They know that they can never go beyond Love's care.

With these spiritual facts Christian Science strips error of its claim of zones wherein to annul the laws of harmony, restrict the action of man, and menace the universal peace. There is no occasion for evil in immeasurable good, no breeding time for paganism, no room for animal magnetism, no tract for war, no place for pestilence, no region for captivity, no chance for discord, sin, or death.

In order that humanity may be aware of man's forever safety in the universe of Soul, Mrs. Eddy has given to the world the revelation of divine Science. In her poem *Christ and Christmas* is a significant statement of this Science:

"Fast circling on, from zone to zone,—
    Bright, blest, afar,—
O'er the grim night of chaos shone
    One lone, brave star.

"In tender mercy, Spirit sped
    A loyal ray
To rouse the living, wake the dead,
    And point the Way—

"The Christ-idea, God anoints—
    Of Truth and Life;
The Way in Science He appoints,
    That stills all strife."

In pondering these words the Christian Science student may become vividly aware of the Christ-power, the true idea of God and His universe, touching all human consciousness to cognizance of God's omnipotence and omnipresence. Neither starting nor stopping, but ever circling on, the Christ challenges one belief after another of error's kingdoms, powers, and accomplishments and ends these beliefs, setting free the helpless, the fearful, the bound. The true idea, appearing wherever error claims to be, proves that only God and His manifestation are there. Rising over "the grim night of chaos," the light of the Christ dispels the darkness of error and "stills all strife" by revealing the undisturbed tranquillity of universal spiritual existence.

"Fast circling on, from zone to zone," the Christ arouses the living to put their trust in God and His eternal plan of goodness. It makes a way of escape for humanity from the beliefs of persecution and captivity, for it demonstrates the eternal unity of God and man, and this truth defies and conquers the lie that men can be isolated from divine help. It quickens men to resist the arrogance of mortal mind and to become aware of angels, God's thoughts, with them to deliver to the uttermost.

The Christ is the deliverer of men both before and after the claim of death may have asserted itself. It is the master of the beliefs of battle and the grave. It is the Saviour of many, the deliverer of masses, the swift, coincident message and manifestation of eternal Life to all men. No edicts, walls, guards, circumstances, or localities can shut out the Christ from anyone. The true idea is inseparable from men, an ever-present influence in human thought, a supreme and timely Saviour possessing adequate power to disprove and dispel every claim of evil to have reality, presence, or power anywhere in God's universe. Of the Christ it can never be said that there is too little or that it is too late to meet human need.

The true idea of one infinite God, good, storms the citadels of paganism and compels the collapse of belief in other gods. Before its flaming light the flimsy structures of mysticism, superstition, imagination, and imposition fade into obscurity. The Christ ends their mesmerism and abolishes their slavery. It is indeed an active Saviour at hand for all mankind.

The Christ is the message and evidence to all men of infinite Love's ever-presence and all-embracement. It brings the realization of the height of Love reaching beyond the heavens, above the stars, over the winds. Up and up as far as thought can go, Love is still the Most High. Soaring cannot pass the borders of its care, nor lose the law of its enfolding.

The Christ reveals the depth of Love. Below the horizon, beneath the waters, under all formation, the foundation of all the creation of Truth, abides Love. Deeper than human reasoning can go, immeasurably beyond the line of exploration, far below the soundings and diggings of human research, at the very center of the universe is Love.

The Christ shows the breadth of Love. Across all waters and over all lands, beyond all space and time, never ceasing, never absent, here and hereafter, stretches the breadth of Love. Worlds upon worlds turn in its grasp, and the tiniest identity of Life is nourished in its bosom. On and on in endless being, Love lives and knows and keeps its own.

As human consciousness beholds this infinitude of Love, God, and His spiritual universe, the claims of hate, war, and desolation draw to a close, for they can have no kingdom, or mandate, where Love is known to be. The zoning of human belief which would give locality and freedom to evil becomes obsolete, and the omnipresence of divine good appears as reality.

God, the creator of all, is at peace, and His universe is thriving in that peace. Throughout the realm of reality there is no danger zone, no war zone; there is no area where evil abides, or operates; there is no barren shore, no waste place, no treacherous depth, no uninhabited space, no prison wall, no fearsome power, no enemy land. Then let us know no fear. Let us walk abroad in safety and win the victory over belief in any power apart from God. In *Science and Health with Key to the Scriptures* (p. 520) Mrs. Eddy says: "The depth, breadth, height, might, majesty, and glory of infinite Love fill all space. That is enough!"

—*Julia M. Johnston*

THE FULLNESS OF JOY

*A*re you known by your joy? This is a question we may well ask ourselves from time to time. The Psalmist wrote of God, "In thy presence is fulness of joy; at thy right hand there are pleasures for evermore" (Ps. 16:11).

Where is God's presence? Is it here, but not there? Was it yesterday, but not today? No. God is everywhere present and is all the time present. So the fullness of joy is everywhere and all the time. If we seem to be without joy, we need to become more spiritually aware of the presence of God.

Christian Science makes practical God's omnipresence and the coexistence of God and man as Mind and its idea. Our Leader, Mary Baker Eddy, says in *Miscellaneous Writings*, "The 'I' will go to the Father when meekness, purity, and love, informed by divine Science, the Comforter, lead to the one God: then the ego is found not in matter but in Mind, for there is but one God, one Mind; and man will then claim no mind apart from God." And she adds, "Idolatry, the supposition of the existence of many minds and more than one God, has repeated itself in all manner of subtleties through the entire centuries, saying as in the beginning, 'Believe in me, and I will make you as gods;' that is, I will give you a separate mind from God (good), named evil; and this so-called mind shall open your eyes and make you know evil, and thus become material, sensual, evil. But bear in mind that a serpent said that; therefore that saying came not from Mind, good, or Truth" (pp. 195–196).

Just as there is only the one God, so there would claim to be the one devil, the serpent, operating in various ways to make us believe that we can be thrust from the presence of God and lose our joy. But whatever the joyless claim may be—whether lack, sorrow, discordant relationships, or disease—we must "bear in mind that a serpent said that."

If a child threw a stone at us, we would deal with the child, not the stone. So, when some joyless circumstance arises, we need to resist the temptation behind it—the temptation to believe in separation from God, the source of all good and all fullness of joy.

We are apt to think that depression is caused by this circumstance or that, but depression is the venom that the serpent, or aggressive mental suggestion, injects into consciousness. It starts its victim ruminating, and then the door is open for destructive thoughts of self-pity and self-centeredness. At the first suggestion of rumination, we need to wake ourselves up.

And how do we keep ourselves from rumination? By doing the opposite. And what is the opposite? Communion. Communion with divine Love, whose children we are. Communion is observed and preserved through the Christ. A part of the office of the Christ, as set forth by Isaiah, is "to appoint unto them that mourn in Zion, to give unto them beauty for ashes, the oil of joy for mourning, the garment of praise for the spirit of heaviness; that they might be called trees of righteousness, the planting of the Lord, that he might be glorified" (Isa. 61:3).

Let us ask ourselves whether we are turning to the Christ or to the serpent. If we turn to the Christ, we can be sure that we shall receive the "oil of joy," and gratitude will flood our being—gratitude for spiritual facts in spite of material seeming, gratitude for our spiritual birthright of freedom, gratitude for the simple, uncomplicated, all-powerful truths of being.

Paul and Silas expressed gratitude when they were cast into prison. They wasted not a moment ruminating and did not confine themselves to praying, but also sang praises, and they did it at midnight.

Let us remember to do the same at our midnight hour, and we also shall enjoy their reward, for we read, "Suddenly there was a great earthquake, so that the foundations of the prison were shaken: and immediately all the doors were opened, and every one's bands were loosed" (Acts 16:26). As we patiently, persistently, and above all, joyfully maintain the spiritual facts of being, the foundations of our prison, whether it is a prison of lack, sorrow, or disease, will be shaken, and not only shall we be free, but also others suffering from the same belief may find the door to freedom open.

Joy is the strong wing which bears us beyond the chaos of mortal mind's imprisoned bewilderment and into the cosmos of spiritual freedom.

Joy is the light which shines out from each experience we encounter; it cannot be hid, but is seen and shared. It is the part of an experience which we can share with others. Nobody can plumb the depths of an experience which is ours alone. Nobody can share with us the battles with temptation, or the holy communings with God, or trace with us the patient steps of heart-searching and self-renunciation which bring us through the wilderness and out of the desert. But the joy which is ours in such experiences cannot be hid. When Moses came from talking with God, his face was shining, because in God's presence there is "fulness of joy."

Our Leader promises us, "Remember, thou canst be brought into no condition, be it ever so severe, where Love has not been before thee and where its tender lesson is not awaiting thee" (*The First Church of Christ, Scientist, and Miscellany*, pp. 149–150). So there is no experience, be it ever so severe, that can separate us from joy, because there is no experience which can separate us from God. This is a spiritual, incontrovertible fact.

— *Rosemary C. Cobham*

God's Law of Adjustment

*M*an lives by divine decree. He is created, governed, supported, and controlled in accord with the law of God. Law means or implies a rule that is established and maintained by power; that which possesses permanence and stability; that which is unchanging, unyielding, and continuous—"the same yesterday, and to-day, and for ever" (Heb. 13:8). The efficiency of law rests entirely in the power that enforces it. A law (so called) that is incapable of being enforced is not law and bears no relationship to law. God is the only creator, the only lawmaker. "All things were made by him; and without him was not any thing made that was made" (John 1:3). All the power, action, intelligence, life, and government in the universe belong to God and have always belonged to Him. He is the Supreme Ruler and does not share His power with another.

Paul said, "The law of the Spirit of life in Christ Jesus hath made me free from the law of sin and death" (Rom. 8:2). So too we know that "the law of the Spirit of life" frees us from "the law of sin and death." Why? Because all the power there is, is on the side of the law of Life, and that which is opposed to this law of Life is not law at all; it is only belief. In other words, every law of God has behind it infinite power to enforce it, while the so-called law of sin and death has no foundation, has nothing back of it that it can depend upon.

When we understandingly declare that the law of God is present and is in operation, we have invoked or brought into action the whole law and the power of God. We have declared the truth, God's truth—and that truth of God is the law of annihilation, obliteration, and elimination to everything that is unlike Him. When we have stated this truth, and applied it, as taught in Christian Science, to any discordant belief with which we are confronted, we have done all that we can do and all that is necessary for us to do in the destruction of any manifestation of error that ever claimed to exist. Error, which has no place in divine Mind, claims to exist in human thought. When we have put it out of human thought, we have driven it out of the only place where it ever pretended to have a foothold, and thereafter to us it becomes nothing.

There is a law of God that is applicable to every conceivable phase of human experience, and no situation or condition can present itself to mortal thought which can possibly exist outside of the direct influence of this infinite law. The effect of the operation of law is always to correct and govern, to harmonize and adjust. Whatever is out of order or discordant can have no basic Principle of its own, but must come under the direct government of God through what may be termed God's law of adjustment. We are not responsible for the carrying out of this law. In fact, we can do nothing in any way to increase, stimulate, or intensify the action or operation of divine Mind, since it is constantly present, always operative, and never ceases to assert and declare itself when rightly appealed to. All we have to do is scientifically to bring this law of adjustment into contact with our unfinished problem, and when we have done this we have performed our full duty. Someone may say, "How can the law of God, operating mentally, affect my problem, which is physical?" This is easily understood when it is realized that the problem is not physical but mental. First we must know that all is Mind and that there is no such thing as matter, and thus exclude from thought the offending material sense.

The original definition of the word *disease* is lack of ease—discomfort, uneasiness, trouble, disquiet, annoyance, injury. "Disease," says Mary Baker Eddy, the Discoverer and Founder of Christian Science, "is an image of thought externalized. The mental state is called a material state. Whatever is cherished in mortal mind as the physical condition is imaged forth on the body" (*Science and Health with Key to the Scriptures*, p. 411). This also applies to heat, cold, hunger, poverty, or any form of discord, all of which are mental, though mortal mind regards them as material states. It can therefore be easily seen how the law of God, which is mental, can be applied to a physical problem.

In reality, the problem is not physical, but purely mental, and is the direct result of some thought cherished in mortal mind. If a man were drowning in mid-ocean with apparently no human help at hand, there is a law of God which, when rightly appealed to, would bring about his rescue. Does the reader doubt this? Then he must believe that it is possible for man to find himself in a condition where God cannot help him. If one were in a burning building or a railroad accident, or if he were in a den of lions, there is a law of God which could at once adjust the apparent material circumstances so as to bring about his complete deliverance.

It is not necessary for us to know in each individual case just what this law of God is, nor how it is going to operate, and an attempted investigation into the why and wherefore might only serve to interfere with its operation and hinder the demonstration. Any fear on our part, occasioned by the fact that divine Mind does not know of our plight, or that infinite wisdom lacks the intelligence necessary to bring about a rescue, should be instantly put out of thought. In *Science and Health with Key to the Scriptures,* Mrs. Eddy writes, "The divine Mind, which forms the bud and blossom, will care for the human body, even as it clothes the lily; but let no mortal interfere with God's government by thrusting in the laws of erring, human concepts" (p. 62). The trouble with us usually is that we want to know just how God is going to help us and when the good results are to be experienced; then we will pass judgment upon it and decide whether we are ready to trust our case in His hands.

Let us see, then, where God's law of adjustment operates. God has no need of being adjusted. The only place where there is any demand for adjustment is in human consciousness; but unless human consciousness appeals to the divine law, unless it is willing and ready to lay down its own sense of human will and stop human planning, put aside human pride, ambition, and vanity, there is no room for the law of adjustment to operate.

When we in our helplessness reach the point where we see we are unable of ourselves to do anything, and then call upon God to aid us; when we are ready to show our willingness to abandon our own plans, our own opinions, our own sense of what ought to be done under the circumstances, and have no fear as to the consequences—then God's law will take possession of and govern the whole situation. We cannot expect, however, that this law will operate in our behalf if we indulge any preconceived ideas as to how it should do its work. We must completely abandon our own view of things and say, "Not my will, but thine, be done" (Luke 22:42). If this step is taken with confidence and a full trust that God is capable of taking care of every circumstance, then no power on earth can prevent the natural, rightful, and legitimate adjustment of all discordant conditions.

This law of adjustment is the universal law of Love, which bestows its blessings on all alike. It does not take from one and give to another. It does not withhold itself under any circumstances, but is ready, and waiting to operate as soon as the invitation is given and human will is set aside. "Whatever holds human thought in line with unselfed love," our Leader says, "receives directly the divine power" (*Science and Health,* p. 192). When we reach the point where we can in confidence and in trust leave everything to the settlement of God's law of adjustment, it will immediately relieve us of all sense of personal responsibility, remove anxiety and fear, and bring peace, comfort, and the assurance of God's protecting care.

The most satisfying and comforting sense of peace and joy always follows the willingness on our part to allow God to control every situation for us through His law of adjustment. When we understand that infinite Mind is the Ruler of the universe, that every idea of God is forever in its proper place, that no condition or circumstance can arise whereby a mistake can find lodgment in God's plan, then we have the complete assurance that God is capable of adjusting everything as it should be. The fact is that all things are already in their rightful place; that no interference or lack of adjustment can really occur. It is only to the unenlightened human sense that there can be any such thing as discord. God's universe is always in perfect adjustment, and all His ideas work together forever in perfect harmony.

When we are willing to give up our frightened and uncertain sense of things and let the divine Mind govern, then and then only shall we behold that "all things work together for good to them that love God" (Rom. 8:28). The discord which seems to be apparent is only what mortal mind believes, whether it be sickness, discomfort, annoyance, or trouble of any kind. When we are willing to relinquish our present views, even though we may believe we are in the right and another in the wrong, we shall not suffer by laying down our human opinions, but rather find that the law of God is ready and active in the right adjustment of everything involved. It may sometimes seem hard when we feel that we are oppressed or imposed upon, to stop resisting, but if our faith in the power of Truth to adjust all things is sufficient, we should be glad of the opportunity to relinquish our claims and place our trust in infinite wisdom, which will adjust everything according to its own unerring law. There is no such thing as failure in the divine Mind. God is never defeated, and those who stand with Him will always receive the benefits of a victory over error.

What then are we to do when we find ourselves involved in a controversy, in a dispute, or in an unpleasant situation of any kind? What are we to do when we have been attacked and maligned, misrepresented or abused? Should we endeavor to return in kind what has been done to us? This would not be appealing to God's law of adjustment. So long as we endeavor to settle the difficulty ourselves, we are interfering with the action of the law of God. Under any circumstance of this kind it will avail us nothing to fight back. We simply show our human weakness when we take the matter into our own hands and attempt either to punish our enemies or to extricate ourselves through any virtue of our own.

When there seem to be two ways of working out a problem in business or in any of the various walks of life, and we decide on a way which seems best, how can we tell, when there are so many arguments against that way, whether the decision is based on Truth or error? Here is a question which can be decided only through the demonstration of God's law of adjustment. There are times when human wisdom is inadequate to tell us just what is the right thing to be done. Under such circumstances we should pray humbly for divine guidance, and then choose that which seems to be in accord with our highest sense of right, knowing that God's law of adjustment regulates and governs all things; and even if we choose the wrong way, we as Christian Scientists have a right to know that God will not allow us to continue in a mistake, but will show us the right way and compel us to walk therein.

When we have reached the point where we are willing to do what seems to us the best and then leave the problem with God, knowing that He will adjust everything according to His unchanging law, we can then withdraw ourselves entirely from the proposition, drop all sense of responsibility, and feel secure in the knowledge that God corrects and governs all things righteously. All we ever need to do is that which is pleasing in the sight of God, that which conforms to divine requirements. If our good is evilly spoken of, this does not affect the situation in any degree, since God does not hold us accountable for the action of others. Our responsibility ceases when we have complied with the demands of good, and there we can afford to let any question rest. It makes no difference how much is at stake or what is involved, if we succeed in getting ourselves out of the way, we can then be satisfied with the words of the prophet: "…the battle is not yours, but God's. … set yourselves, stand ye still, and see the salvation of the Lord" (II Chron. 20:15, 17).

We cannot hope to work out of this human sense of existence without making mistakes. We may make many, but will profit by them all. We are at liberty to change our belief of things as often as we get new light. We should not let our vanity compel us to adhere to a proposition simply because we have taken a stand thereon. We should be willing to relinquish our former views and change our thought on any subject as often as wisdom furnishes us enlightenment.

Christian Scientists are sometimes accused of being changeable. What if they are, if it is always God that changes them? Is a Christian Scientist any less a Scientist because he changes his mind? Is a general less fit to lead his army because in the heat of battle he changes his tactics under the guidance of wisdom? A too determined sense of carrying out a preconceived plan is more likely to be the enthronement of erring human will.

Christian Scientists are minutemen, armed and equipped to respond to any call of wisdom, always ready and willing to abandon personal views or opinions, and to allow that Mind to be in them "which was also in Christ Jesus" (Phil. 2:5).

—Adam H. Dickey

THE GREAT HEART OF INFINITE LOVE

*I*n a poem entitled "Signs of the Heart," Mary Baker Eddy writes in the second stanza (*Poems*, p. 24):

> "O Love divine,
>   This heart of Thine
> Is all I need to comfort mine."

Today, as yesterday, this great heart of Love is expressed in the living, palpitating presence of the healing Christ, revealing the divine nature of God to men. It is restoring the sick, reforming the sinner, and raising the dead through the gentle ministry of Christian Science. As thought becomes spiritualized, this great heart will be understood to be inseparable from the life-giving, animating, creative Principle, God, giving individuality and being to man. Without the governing, controlling power of this great heart, man could not exist for a moment. Since man's coexistence with God is eternal, nothing can sever this divine relationship. In reality, man cannot be dispirited, discouraged, or disheartened, for God has said (Ezek. 11:19), "I will give them one heart, and I will put a new spirit within you."

Someone may say at this point, This is all very beautiful and inspiring, but just what does it mean to me in seeking healing for heart trouble? It means this: that you too can be permanently healed of your heart disease, just as a member of the writer's family was, through the understanding and realization of your individual at-one-ment, as the child of God, with this great, life-giving heart of Love.

This woman had been suffering from a complication of diseases for over ten years, and her heart was badly affected. After exhausting every material means known to her doctors, she turned to Christian Science in desperation and was healed through reading *Science and Health with Key to the Scriptures* by Mrs. Eddy. She often said that when she came to pages 112 to 116 of this textbook, she felt her healing taking place as she saw that Christian Science was demonstrated from the basis of one divine Principle. Her thought opened to the divine law of Love governing man. Her heart trouble fled as she pondered these words by Mrs. Eddy (*ibid.*, p. 113): "The vital part, the heart and soul of Christian Science, is Love. Without this, the letter is but the dead body of Science,—pulseless, cold, inanimate."

If this is true of Christian Science, the woman reasoned, it should be true of those who accept the teachings of Christian Science; and since I have accepted the revelation of Christian Science I begin to see the spiritual fact that what is really vital to me is Love. Through this unfoldment the healing Christ, the manifestation of the living, palpitating presence of Love, annulled the verdict of death, animated and invigorated her with a newness of life and a keen consciousness of God's presence. With a new sense of heart derived from Spirit instead of matter, she proved these spiritual facts for herself, as well as others, in freedom and health for many years. Anyone seeking healing can feel this same vitalizing power permeating his being and restoring his health, for the Bible tells us that God is no respecter of persons. What He does for one, He is ready to do for all.

Thousands of people are being heartened, renewed, regenerated, revitalized, and established through the consciousness of the restoring presence of the Christ. Thus the divine nature of God is being manifested through understanding of the great heart of Love, giving to mankind true motives, right desires, pure affection, joy, happiness, prosperity, and success. By allaying men's fears and destroying the false beliefs which make the body sick and the heart faint, the Christ dispels also the errors of selfishness, such as animosity, rivalry, deceit, dishonesty, jealousy, envy, revenge, and hate.

The heart of humanity is beginning to know its Redeemer through Christian Science. This Science exposes the false action of mortal mind, which governs every function and organ of the material body, and reveals the supremacy of immortal divine Mind as the only power governing God's universe and man. It shows that through the realization of the all-controlling power of God, mortal mind is subjugated and the body becomes harmonious. St. Paul clearly saw the truth that we live in and because of God when he said in that wonderful chapter in Acts (17:25, 28) that God "giveth to all life, and breath, and all things; . . . for in him we live, and move, and have our being."

It must be spiritually perceived and accepted that there is but one God, one Mind, one Soul, governing man and the universe; then spiritual enlightenment reveals spontaneously that there is but one heart—the heart of Love—pulsating, impelling, stimulating, energizing, controlling, and animating man. Its action is perpetual, immutable, inexhaustible, because it is the vitality of Life and Love. All true action and volition proceeds from this divine source, and nothing can interrupt the ever continuous, constant, harmonious action of God, which is individualized in man. There is but one cause and effect, and this fact is the heart of Christianity, uniting in one body all men.

The loving Father is holding His universal family safe from harm in the great heart of infinite Love, ever strengthening and heartening all. The angels of His presence are constantly bringing comfort and assurance to humanity, so that all can unite in saying with Mrs. Eddy,

"O Love divine,
This heart of Thine
Is all I need to comfort mine."

—*Louise Hurford Brown*

HANDLING ANIMAL MAGNETISM IN HEALING

I remember a difficult case I had taken on in the early days of my practice of Christian Science with all the wonderful courage and inspiration that so often characterize those first thrilling days in the healing work, the spirit of which we should never lose.

I had worked long and earnestly on this case, yet it didn't respond as I had expected. One day, feeling the need for greater enlightenment, I called my mother, who was an experienced Christian Science practitioner, and told her impersonally about the case. Her instant reply was, "Have you handled animal magnetism in relation to it?" I said I hadn't thought of doing so, specifically. "Well," she said, "stop handling the claim and its symptoms for tonight. Instead, thoroughly handle animal magnetism with all its bearing on the case."

I pondered what she said. "Surely," I thought, "I have spent days endeavoring to handle the outcome of this material belief of animal magnetism. What more should I be doing?" Then it sharply occurred to me, "Yes, that is exactly what I have been doing—handling the effect of something but not handling the something itself."

I saw with great clarity that the underlying error behind every case of physical disease is the mesmerism that makes us accept, consciously or unconsciously, the basic belief of matter or physicality as the foundation of life. In just handling the claim of disease itself and its symptoms, and even the mortal laws attached to it, we are merely lopping off the branches or effects of this basic error, leaving the belief of the centuries-old underlying cause untouched. Animal magnetism is the human antipode, or opposite, of the divine Science of all healing. It needs to be reduced to its nothingness by specific treatment.

That night I began to handle the basic error called animal magnetism with all its ramifications. First, working with the guidance of *Science and Health with Key to the Scriptures* by Mary Baker Eddy, the Discoverer and Founder of Christian Science, I saw that "animal magnetism has no

scientific foundation, for God governs all that is real, harmonious, and eternal, and His power is neither animal nor human" (*Science and Health*, p. 102). Therefore, nothing that emanates from the belief in animal magnetism has any scientific foundation either. It was clear that only animal magnetism was presenting the picture of a sick person needing treatment, disturbing the patient and her relatives with suggestions of pain and fear—even trying to delude the practitioner that the case had not yet been met by Truth. This was just one ballooned-up error, not a lot of different errors needing handling. And this belief of animal magnetism had not one quality of Truth.

Suddenly I was aware of the power of Truth at work; I knew the way had been swept clean for the healing Christ to have full sway. The patient felt it too, and in a short time she was free. The specific handling of animal magnetism had released the power of Truth in the treatment to demonstrate its supremacy.

This does not mean that there are not countless cases of lovely clear-cut healings going on through almost effortless mental work when there is no resistance against them. Indeed, someone may ask, "Why do we need to handle animal magnetism at all?" Because animal magnetism is a belief so promotive of matter and material creation that it cannot bear any truth that reveals creation as exclusively in and of Spirit. It assumes two specific delusive roles: either it parades as matter substance, matter origin, organic matter, physicality, or it hides as subtle mental resistance to Spirit and everything spiritual. It would argue against the very results we long to bring out. We need to see through its subtlety and destroy its effects.

What are some of the ways in which animal magnetism tries to impede healing?

If an individual is not responding to treatment—to the power of the Christ, Truth, we are entertaining on his behalf—we cannot ignore the claim of an obstructive influence. This obstruction, the carnal mind's enmity against God and against the divine law of Christ-healing operating in our movement, needs to be seen and specifically dealt with.

For example, would it have been enough for Jesus to destroy only the mortal belief of poisoning and pain from the nails that were driven into him, when actually it was hatred of Jesus himself and his teachings by the opponents of Truth that had driven in those nails in the first place? So today we often need specifically to handle hatred against Truth and its revelator before physical healing can be fully brought forth. This particular form of error is one of the carnal mind's most subtle attempts to obstruct the full glory of physical healing in our movement today, and it would deceive the very elect.

It is not surprising that spiritual healing should be the point at which animal magnetism attacks our religion. Our beloved Leader, Mrs. Eddy, writes: "In different ages the divine idea assumes different forms, according to humanity's needs. In this age it assumes, more intelligently than ever before, the form of Christian healing" (*Miscellaneous Writings*, p. 370). This holy idea of spiritual healing, which Mrs. Eddy has established as the cornerstone of her beloved Church, is the most outstanding gift that has come to the world since the coming of Christ Jesus. It is not too much to say that the continuity of our religion and the salvation of the whole world rest on the preservation of this divine idea. Thus it is the carnal mind's attack on our healing work that needs the clearest perception and the most dedicated handling.

We know our Leader's revelation of Truth means the complete destruction of animal magnetism in all its forms. But animal magnetism, symbolized from the beginning as the serpent, still tries to bite the heel of the woman, its destroyer, because its supposititious subtle instinct tells it that the woman, the spiritual idea of Love, will bruise its head, will utterly destroy its so-called intelligence. Therefore, in our healing work it is essential to deal with malpractice against Mrs. Eddy, who represented the divine idea, as an important part of our counteracting the animal magnetism operating against the healing Truth itself. I am deeply convinced that bringing our Leader's name and place more into the front line of our practice and handling the world's resistance against her divine mission can do more to facilitate good and quick healing than any other single factor.

To illustrate: I know of a woman who was healed of severe arthritis after being crippled, unable to walk, for many months. The practitioner had been praying to see that no phase of animal magnetism could close her own eyes to what still needed to be handled. She was led to offer the woman one of the books entitled *We Knew Mary Baker Eddy* and met a sharp rejection. "No, thank you," said the patient. "I don't like hearing about Mrs. Eddy as a person."

This immediately showed the practitioner the resistance the Christian Science treatment had been up against. Trusting in the woman's spiritual ability to perceive the truth, she cut right across this resistance. They talked for an hour about Mrs. Eddy, and when the practitioner got up to go, the patient walked with her to the door. Within a week she was out shopping. The healing was complete and permanent.

This woman had dearly loved the message in our textbook but never loved the messenger. It took this handling of the resistance to the messenger to dissolve the hardness in her thought that had held up the healing for so long.

Animal magnetism is, in belief, a most versatile actor. It will parade itself in incredible disguises, aiming to draw thought away from the main issue. It can pose not only as the patient's own fretfulness but as pressure from frightened relatives, or as the hidden irritation of the one having to care for him.

These are not really difficult people or circumstances but concealed animal magnetism, mental decoys to divert the direct healing power of the Christ, Truth, from reaching the patient. Our Leader gives us a helpful statement on this in her *Message to The Mother Church for 1901*. She says, "People may listen complacently to the suggestion of the inaudible falsehood, not knowing what is hurting them or that they are hurt." Then she states with assurance "This mental bane could not bewilder, darken, or misguide consciousness, physically, morally, or spiritually, if the individual knew what was at work and his power over it" (p. 20). What a wonderful help to our healing work is this perceptive unveiling of error by our Leader, so that we now do know what is at work and—most important of all—through God's love, *our* power over it!

One thing is important. Practitioners or nurses should never allow themselves to become impatient with these environmental forms of animal magnetism, however trying they may be. Sometimes the patient's attitude toward these very difficulties may enable the practitioner to discern the mental causes underlying the physical problem. Then he can handle dispassionately and compassionately just what needs to be dealt with, never minding the extra requirements that compel him to be more specific and thorough in the application of Truth and Love.

It is interesting that when Jesus went to heal Jairus' daughter, he didn't tell the maid to arise until he had thoroughly coped with the in-crowding arguments of animal magnetism surrounding the case. "He put them all out" (Luke 8:54). Had he not first silenced these disturbances, the young girl could not have heard the divine call to life and responded to it. Hence the practitioner's first need is to silence all intrusive arguments, so that the still small voice of scientific treatment and divine Love can be clearly heard by the one needing resuscitation.

It is noteworthy that our Master did visit this and many other cases in his healing ministry. Animal magnetism should never be allowed to delude a practitioner into thinking there is no necessity to visit certain cases, when it may be needful for the protection of the patient and of our Cause that he give this outward evidence of professional attention. He may need to observe the relative seriousness of the pressures of mortal mind against the case and any special requirements for human care. He may even need to rouse the patient with the audible voice of Truth. Many a patient's heart has been strengthened for healing by feeling the love that prompted a practitioner's visit!

We should never play into the hands of animal magnetism by failing to give a case the full measure of spiritual care it needs, especially if a patient is not improving. The patient's thought should never be allowed to become frightened or discouraged through the feeling that his case is not understood. At such a point animal magnetism could argue to him that he needs a doctor's diagnosis. Such suggestions are actually projected malpractice against the power of the healing Christ, and not the patient's thoughts at all. Christ is the entirely adequate healer; and, as Jesus showed us, "lie" and "liar" are specific enough names to challenge and destroy every disease.

I have mentioned in this article some of the subtleties of animal magnetism that would try to impede the lovely healings of which our beloved Church is capable. When challenged instantly and thoroughly by Truth, they are powerless. They cannot touch or hinder a single case of healing that may come our way, because through our Leader's great love for humanity, we now know exactly what is at work and our complete power over it.

So, let us go forth, knowing with divine assurance that, even if the material lie does still try to make war on the spiritual idea of healing, it can only impel us all to rise to the full height of demonstration, destroying every argument that would oppose itself against our knowledge of God. Thus we shall show the world the full physical effect of the Christ-healing going on in its midst through the power of Christian Science.

This is the divine and exhilarating call to each of us in our healing work today.

—*E. Vera Gorringe Plimmer*

HEALING THE "INCURABLE"

In these times, the forces of publicity about certain diseases have been intensified through radio and television, as well as the press. Some of them have the label "incurable," and this label is sometimes in the forefront of the unwittingly injurious publicity.

But by the power of God, Truth, as understood in Christian Science, the label of incurability has been stripped off diseases previously typed as unhealable. Everyone can scientifically utilize that power now to overcome persistent illness. Christian Science has brought new insights into the nature of disease, and these are accompanied by explanations of the spiritual means of healing it.

Christian Science denominates disease as a claim, the claim that there is something opposed to the harmony and painlessness that characterize Soul, God, and that belong unendingly to Soul's reflection, man. In this sense, disease is not an actual physical condition that is either curable or incurable. In scientifically absolute terms, disease is a "curse causeless" (Prov. 26:2) and is without evidence, without history, without future.

Mary Baker Eddy states emphatically in *Science and Health with Key to the Scriptures*, "There is *no disease*" (p. 421). Hence so-called incurable disease is the claim that some nothings are temporary and some are permanent. This may sound odd, and it is. But in the light of the Science of Mind-healing, incurability is more than odd. It is impossible.

When we speak of incurability, we're talking about a mortal belief, not about a genuine state of affairs. The belief is as inaccurate as was the once universally held belief that the earth is flat. Incurability is a suggestion that derives from mortal mind, having the effect of striking anxiety into our hearts, and in this way deflecting us from entertaining the reality of God's power and allness.

If the divine healing Principle works in one instance—and it has worked in numberless thousands of cases—then it has the capability of healing in all instances in which it is understandingly applied and unresistingly accepted. On the other hand, if we accept incurability as a fact, even in one instance, we deny the whole fabric of Christian Science and its authority in our thought.

Spiritual healing is not the outcome of a battle of powers—the power of God battling with the supposed power of evil and succeeding in some cases only. In Science, power is all on the side of Truth, without any qualifications. And there is no power at all on the side of error. To meet the claim of incurability, we need to be sure that we give total emphasis to the power of Truth, thus according no residue of power to discord.

A progressively spiritual approach to the claim of incurable disease strengthens our confidence in treating it; a totally spiritual approach to incurability imbues us with complete conviction. Total confidence in Truth is the perfect antidote for the supposed incurability of some states of mortal belief. Christian Science gives us the highest justification for unreserved conviction.

As we reason under the direction of Christian Science, we come to the conclusion that there are only two final options open to us: either God is omnipotent, all-power, or God is restricted in His authority and government, and so not God at all but a myth of a finite deity. Realizing that God, Truth, is indeed omnipotent, we establish perfect grounds for full confidence and conviction. This realization tips out uncertainty from our thought and cancels our incurability.

Additional confidence in dealing with what is labeled a hopeless case comes from an understanding that we are working under law and not with chance. Success is not speculative but sure.

These days, aircraft designers are so confident of their grasp of the laws of flight, of aerodynamics, and of physics generally that they design planes with full assurance that they will fly.

When Christ Jesus walked on the water, he had a full comprehension of and reliance on spiritual law as giving man dominion over the sense of a physical environment. He knew clearly that spiritual law is higher than apparent physical law, and that consequently he could do all that he really needed to do in particular circumstances—including walking on the water. He didn't wonder whether or not he could walk on the waves but understood why he could. Peter wondered, and sank.

In treating the so-called incurable problem we

need complete assurance that we're working with God's law—His law of permanent health for man. This law, understood, gives us dominion over claims, suggestions, beliefs, appearances, and over matter-based diagnoses and prognoses. The perceptive study of the Bible and the writings of Mary Baker Eddy, the Discoverer and Founder of Christian Science, combined with the living of what we learn there, gives us this certainty of divine lawfulness that overrules a lower sense of law.

Mortal mind has no changeless laws belonging to it, no laws it can apply. Problems labeled incurable are not backed up by actual law, and we need not be intimidated by the supposed laws of medicine or pathology or whatever. All law belongs to divine Principle. No law really attaches to material conditions of any kind to produce either unhealable sin or unhealable disease.

Consequently, in dealing with such a claim, *Science and Health* advises: "Dismiss it with an abiding conviction that it is illegitimate, because you know that God is no more the author of sickness than He is of sin. You have no law of His to support the necessity either of sin or sickness, but you have divine authority for denying that necessity and healing the sick" (p. 390).

Each of us needs to handle the mesmeric claim of incurability regularly. And the claim is best quashed before it has seemed to manifest itself as an aspect of a problem. This is soundly done by clearly understanding the nothingness, the illusive nature, of disease itself, thus leaving nothing for the label of incurableness to adhere to. Disease, in belief, is just as much a mental state as is fear, its usual precondition. If disease were a material objective reality—termed either curable or incurable—it would not be within the scope of spiritually mental activity.

The supposititious resister of spiritual healing is animal magnetism. Animal magnetism argues that there really is life and intelligence in matter, that man is in matter, and that nothing can be done about it. Should we concede this point to it, mortal mind may then try to argue its case from instances of apparent failure of Truth to heal. This argument can only seem plausible to a materialized view of man, and unless we annul it, we may find ourselves thinking, "I knew somebody who had something that is supposed to be incurable, and who tried to overcome it spiritually, and I heard that they failed. Then, are some conditions incurable—even in Science?"

We must get down to fundamentals and strip the disguise from this misleading line of thought. Under the analysis of the Science of being, seeming failures are disclosed as passing mesmeric pictures, not actualities. If we're tempted by this particular line of mortal reasoning, we might ask ourselves, "Am I going to believe God, or am I going to believe material sense?"

It's material sense that insists that man is mortal, open to disease, illness, decay, death. Material sense lies. We don't have to believe its lies. In fact, we must be absolutely sure that we're not believing one of its lies. If, weakly, we believe in failure instead of challenging it on spiritual grounds, next time we give a treatment to ourselves or another we may not do as well as previously.

Christian Science is scientific. Our job is to conform our thought to Truth and to divine law, not to erratic human beliefs and images of mortality. Our job is not to fuss with pictures and shadows, no matter how real-seeming, but to know the truth and go on knowing it, in spite of what mortal mind is trying to depict as the reality.

The desire for more thorough and complete healing doesn't demand anything that we're not able to meet through genuine dedication. God will sustain our effort. The Bible assures us, "Draw nigh to God, and he will draw nigh to you" (James 4:8). A seeming failure is not a time to doubt but a time to cultivate more conviction. A temporarily inadequate demonstration is not an occasion to despair but an opportunity to rise nearer to God. How? In the strength of Spirit. Understanding man, hence our real being, to be the reflection of Mind, we have the ability to transcend the argument of failure, and nothing can take away that ability.

To approach the so-called incurable with more assurance, we need to be clear what is going on, metaphysically, in healing. The outward sense of Christian Science practice is that a human being, endowed with a certain amount of spirituality and scientific understanding, is mentally treating someone else, some place else, who has an inadequate sense of God and His goodness and has some kind of problem because of it. We must look further, into the realism of the practice.

Mrs. Eddy writes, "Mind in every case is the eternal God, good" (*Science and Health*, p. 415). This implies—human judgment notwithstanding—that there is truly no suffering, materialized, fearful, self-centered patient's mind in the case. Nor is there any tentative, struggling, limitedly spiritualized practitioner's mind in the case. But Mind, in every instance, is the eternal Mind, God. Though the human picture presents a practitioner helping a patient with an apparently resistant problem, what is really taking place, now and everywhere, is the one divine Mind knowing and glorying in its infinitude, perfection, and beauty, and holding man perpetually in its care.

In the realm of Mind and its idea—and in truth there is no other realm—there is no uncertain practitioner and no unresponding patient believing in incurability; but divine Mind is completely All, and is maintaining its allness, knowing no challenge. God and His allness is the essence, the substance, the beginning and the end, of the events that we describe humanly as Christian Science treatment and its resultant healing.

In this fully spiritual sense of the practice there are no real problems either curable or incurable; hence, neither successes nor failures. There are neither spiritualized nor materialized local consciousnesses. There is just the one divine consciousness, the eternal divine Ego.

Ultimately speaking, the claim of incurability doesn't have to be put out of consciousness, for the divine consciousness is the only actual consciousness, either of the practitioner or the patient. And by its very nature it always was and is impervious to all error. Error does not belong to consciousness, nor does consciousness belong to error, ever. Consciousness belongs to Mind, God, always.

Christian Science is profoundly encouraging. It is the Comforter promised by Christ Jesus. What could be more comforting than the revelation that God's man is flawless, sinless, diseaseless, now—especially when this revelation is accompanied by the explanation of its potential application by everyone willing to follow its leadings? To the Christ, the spiritual presence and power of God, there is no hopeless case, and we can begin proving so today.

—*Geoffrey J. Barratt*

I SEE!

In her textbook, *Science and Health with Key to the Scriptures*, Mary Baker Eddy, the Discoverer and Founder of Christian Science, links healing with light. Light and healing—these terms are practically synonymous, for Mrs. Eddy does not here refer to solar light, but to the light of spiritual discernment or understanding. To speak of having light upon a situation usually means that the truth regarding the situation has been made clear. When the truth regarding a discordant condition is made clear to us in the light of Christian Science, that condition is healed. In the study of this Science we find that spiritual understanding brings healing—healing by means of seeing the spiritual fact regarding any situation. This accords with Paul's definition of light (Eph. 5:13) as "whatsoever doth make manifest." And when the truth is made manifest to us, we say, "I see!"

A student of optics has to take as groundwork a course in physics on light. Every optical problem presented to him has light as its basis of solution. Light is an essential part of every optical problem. A study of the Christian Science textbook shows that its author was familiar with the theories of physical optics, for in many cases she uses optical phenomena to illustrate some spiritual truth. This will readily be seen by looking up such terms as "camera," "focal distance," "inverted image," "lens," "retina," and so on, in a Concordance to her works.

It is significant to find that our Leader, despite her knowledge of physical optics, does not concede finality or reality to any of the stated laws thereof. A reference to *Science and Health* (pp. 503-511) will show that she discovered the true nature and origin of light to be entirely spiritual, and that her conclusions regarding optics are from the standpoint of that light which, as she writes on page 510, "is a symbol of Mind, of Life, Truth, and Love, and not a vitalizing property of matter."

In dealing with what are called optical problems, or conditions of impaired human sight, the only conclusion we can arrive at, in the light of Christian Science, is that the physical organs called "eyes" have very little to do with the problem. Jesus, who possessed more truly scientific knowledge than any man who has ever trod this earth, implied that with the physical eyes we do not really see when he said (Mark 8:18), "Having eyes, see ye not?"

Mrs. Eddy makes this clear in her article entitled "There is no Matter" on page 31 of *Unity of Good*. She points out regarding the question of sight that the belief of mankind is that it sees matter with matter, but this is impossible, for matter is of itself incapable of any sense of sight. That which seems to make matter capable of seeing is what Christian Science terms mortal mind, the human or carnal mind, which Paul says is "enmity against God"; in other words, it is a contradiction of the divine Mind. How contradictory are mortal theories, which state that although the human so-called mind is superior to matter it is nevertheless entirely dependent upon matter for its sense of sight, and that both are in turn dependent upon a third material element called physical light!

Is it not reasonable, then, that we should discard this contradictory theory of sight, and look for that which is the unalterable, indestructible basis of true vision? Mortal belief in optical defects or disease of the eyes does not affect man's real sight, for the truth is that man is image, reflection, one with his divine source, God. Light and its rays may be likened to Mind and its ideas. We do not, therefore, in truth, need rays of solar light in order to see; neither is true vision dependent upon the correct focusing of these rays by the lenses and various muscular actions of the human eyes, for "the rays of infinite Truth, when gathered into the focus of ideas, bring light instantaneously, whereas a thousand years of human doctrines, hypotheses, and vague conjectures emit no such effulgence" (*Science and Health*, p. 504).

Mind is All; therefore there is nothing outside of Mind which perceives or can be perceived. There is nothing outside of infinite Mind which can be projected or expressed. As Mrs. Eddy states (*ibid.*, p. 126), "Human thought never projected the least portion of true being." Man, the idea of Mind, is the embodiment of all right ideas. He includes vision, perception, and the power to express them. Man is the compound idea of infinite Mind and expresses God's infinite self-containment. Therefore any belief of bodily disorder, faulty action, sin, or disease is false because it claims that there is something besides the expression of infinite Principle, and that because Mind is all-seeing it must necessarily see imperfection. But because Mind sees only what it expresses within itself, the conclusion is that disease or discord of any kind is nonexistent, neither seen nor expressed; it is a false suggestion that vision can be material and become faulty.

Mind sees, and man is the expression of the

all-seeing Mind, the individualized evidence of the seeing of this Mind. Man, as a compound idea, includes within himself the faculty of vision. It is not from without. As Christian Scientists we are all learning to see, learning to claim our identity as man. Paul wrote (II Cor. 5:7), "We walk by faith, not by sight." Man sees from the standpoint of the reflection of Mind, Life, Truth, and Love. With this standpoint of vision, then, let us see to it that our images are perfect and clear images of Truth, and that we do not see imperfections, which Love never made. This we so often do when we rely on a material sense of sight and see around us those who seem to be imperfect—lame, diseased, depraved, ill-tempered, and so on. It was Jesus' correct view of man which healed the sick. Let us have this correct view, considering all things from a spiritual standpoint rather than from a material one; then our eyes cannot dictate to us what we see or do not see.

I once met a little girl who presented to the physical senses a condition of extreme mental dullness, together with an optical difficulty which claimed that her eyes were useless. A few years later the same child, after being in the care of Christian Scientists, presented an entirely different picture. She was bright, charming, unusually intelligent, could see perfectly even at a distance, and was accomplished at drawing, painting, and fine work. But at that time her eyes were in the same condition as when I had previously seen her, showing no sign of performing their natural functions. She was literally seeing without the use of her eyes. The natural sequence to this would be that her eyes would eventually become normal, and inquiry a few months later revealed that the eyes were functioning more and more naturally. It had been proved that the physical organs performed their natural function because of what the child spiritually saw concerning true vision.

Sometimes mortals believe that age produces difficulty in the focusing of the physical eye, because of a change in the human muscular system. If we consider this belief fearlessly, we shall see how ridiculous it is. True vision does not depend upon the muscles or any material element; neither does it depend upon how long we have been believing in a material existence, in a material world. The belief of deterioration of sight is the exact opposite of what we ought logically to expect. It would be more reasonable to assert that as men and women progress in spiritual understanding their vision should become more acute, as indeed it does.

Strictly speaking, the condition of impaired vision, so called, is not one of the individual's "age" but of the world-wide belief in the passage of time. The problem of spectacles for reading does not begin at a certain advanced age; it begins with birth. The whole of our human problems can be traced to the beliefs that we were born at a certain date, that we live in a material world during a certain passage of time, and that we then die. It is reported that Jesus once said, "I am come to destroy the works of birth."

When we can see clearly that man was never born, but always is the manifestation of Life, and therefore is not subject to the belief of passage of time, we shall quite naturally and manifestly, as Jesus did, overcome the various beliefs which argue that man must die. The only thing which can die is the belief that man has lived in or experienced any claims of matter. There never has been a time when an apple would not drop to the ground if allowed to fall. But it is comparatively recently in the world's history that this fact led Newton to discover the law of gravity, though apples have always been subject to this law.

So it is with true vision. There has never been a time when man has not been in possession of the perfect faculty of infinite vision. It is not and has never been true that man can be limited by shortsightedness, or that he is unable to discern the glorious infinitude of the spiritual universe, in which he lives. Neither is it true, nor has it ever been, that man needs to overcome farsightedness in order to discern the glories of Soul, which are close at hand. The discernment of this fact spiritualizes thought and lets in the light of Truth.

If some people believe they find glasses a temporary aid to physical sight, we can be grateful that such use is, at the most, only the addition of one form of human belief to another, the belief in the use of lenses as an aid to the belief of material eyesight. Neither physical eyes nor glass lenses ever touch the real sense of vision, which is wholly spiritual, and glasses can do no more harm or good than belief permits. True vision is not dependent upon the use of the eyes; neither is it dependent upon the use of glasses, lotions, or other material aids; nor can it be hindered by them. Any supposed action resulting from the use of material aids can only be in the realm of belief and certainly is not in Truth.

With what authority and fearlessness we can claim that here and now man is free from any defect or lack of vision! Real vision lies in the exercise of Mind-qualities—love, joy, poise, truthfulness, gratitude, obedience, and the like. Against such there is no optical law. As our Master said (Matt. 5:8), "Blessed are the pure in heart: for they shall see God"—shall find themselves identified with the images formed by infinite Mind, Love.

—*Noel D. Bryan-Jones*

"I WAS THERE"

"The Lord possessed me in the beginning of his way. . . . When he prepared the heavens, I was there. . . . Then I was by him, as one brought up with him: and I was daily his delight, rejoicing always before him" (Prov. 8:22–30). These are words of wisdom from the book of Proverbs. But how aptly may one utter them in recognition and acknowledgment of man's preexistence and coexistence with his creator.

Before we came into Christian Science, many of us probably accepted the belief, general among Christians, that life begins for us here and that we can look forward to spiritual immortality hereafter. Christian Science shows us that anything which has a beginning must have an ending and that which is immortal must be eternally immortal.

To unillumined thinking, the idea of preexistence can bring with it little spiritual comfort or inspiration. What can be known, or even theorized, about this idea by mortals if their thought can only go back to monkeys and molecules or to transmigration? However, in Christian Science the revelation of God, Principle, as the true origin, cause, and governing law of man and the universe brings to light spiritual causation and the eternal continuity of perfect effect.

As Christian Scientists we acknowledge one infinite God as the only cause and creator, and man as His effect. Therefore all cause must be Spirit, and effect spiritual. Infinite Mind being all-inclusive, there can be nothing outside of it. Everything included in infinity, untouched by time and space limitations, always was, is, and ever will be. Infinity never began. Thus there never was a time when individual man, as a complete and perfect idea of infinite Mind, did not exist. He did not have to be made out of nothing. To understand this correctly is to understand something of preexistence.

It is very important for us intelligently to acknowledge our preexistence; in fact, it is as important as to acknowledge our immortality. Preexistence is included in our immortality: it is part of it. Jesus did not say, "Before Abraham was, I was." No. He said (John 8:58), "Before Abraham was, I am." He knew the continuity of his true being and could say (John 8:14), "I know whence I came, and whither I go."

Mary Baker Eddy says in *Miscellaneous Writings* (p. 189), "The meek Nazarene's steadfast and true knowledge of preexistence, of the nature and the inseparability of God and man,—made him mighty." Have we, any of us, sufficient "steadfast and true knowledge of preexistence, of the nature and the inseparability of God and man" which makes mighty? If not, why not? The power is always in the spiritual right idea, and this right idea of the true knowledge concerning preexistence and the coexistence and inseparability of God and man is revealed to us in Christian Science now. Is it not imperative for us to ponder this and lay hold of that which can bring us newness of life, great comfort, encouragement, and joyful inspiration?

In *Science and Health with Key to the Scriptures* Mrs. Eddy states (p. 557), "Divine Science rolls back the clouds of error with the light of Truth, and lifts the curtain on man as never born and as never dying, but as coexistent with his creator." "Never born," "coexistent with his creator"! If we do not recognize what that means in relation to our preexistence, we are surely leaving something which needs to be recognized.

Anyone who does not know enough about preexistence to acknowledge and accept it with joy must have as yet a very incomplete concept of his immortal being and therefore cannot rejoice in that glory which Jesus had with the Father "before the world was" (John 17:5). If we did not have that glory with God in our preexistence, we can never have it. Our Father-Mother God, the infinite divine Love which is changeless Principle, knows no variableness or shadow of turning.

Let us refer again to that rousing challenge to us all—to come out of the darkness of materiality into the glorious light which reveals the splendor of our immortal being. "Divine Science rolls back the clouds of error with the light of Truth, and lifts the curtain on man as never born and as never dying, but as coexistent with his creator." How marvelous to have that curtain lifted, that veil swept away, and to know ourselves, our true, immortal selfhood, as coexistent with our creator! Divine Science reveals this coexistence to us today, for our enlightenment, encouragement, and joyous freedom. Let us claim it, demonstrate it.

Never born and never dying—that is the truth regarding man, and to understand and demonstrate it, we must go back to man's preexistence and claim all that belongs to it. We must claim the continuity of the perfection which belongs to each one of us as the perpetual reflection of perfect Mind, the emanation of divine Love.

To begin rightly is important. So let us ponder spiritual causation and with awe and joyful gratitude demonstrate what an understanding of man's spiritual origin means for us. From that standpoint, each one of us can declare with complete confidence such truths as: "My background, as God's idea or reflection, is wholly satisfactory. I am the effect of spiritual causation alone. My nature, therefore, is wholly spiritual, Godlike, perfect, complete. It always has been, is so now, and always will be. My origin is perfection, and the continuity of this perfection is my immortality."

Mrs. Eddy has shown us that our Master's true vision of man's spiritual, eternal perfection was the basis of his marvelous healing ministry. May we not all feel that it is both comforting and encouraging for us to turn from the false evidence of material sense, ponder man's original and eternal perfection, and identify ourselves and our fellow men with it? Perfection is the truth of our being, and it is mighty!

We must constantly endeavor to see ourselves through the lens of Spirit. How sympathetically our Leader brings this out in *The First Church of Christ, Scientist, and Miscellany* (p. 129): "And how is man, seen through the lens of Spirit, enlarged, and how counterpoised his origin from dust, and how he presses to his original, never severed from Spirit!" To see ourselves, the universe, all things, no longer through "a glass, darkly," but through the lens of Spirit, will surely dissipate the mistiness of the Adam-dream, and the reality of all things will come to light.

The Bible records that out of the whirlwind Job heard the voice of God saying to him (Job 38:3, 4): "I will demand of thee, and answer thou me. Where wast thou when I laid the foundations of the earth? declare, if thou hast understanding." Is not this divine demand uttering itself to us today, asking for a right understanding and acknowledgment of our preexistence and coexistence with our Maker?

As all that is implied in this demand unfolds to our thought, we shall find ourselves able to reply understandingly to that momentous question, "Where wast thou?" with joyous conviction (Job 38:7), "When the morning stars sang together, and all the sons of God shouted for joy,' I was there."

Lord, "I was there"!

—*Violet Hay*

IDENTITY

⁓

The question, "Who am I?" is one which confronts everyone. Indeed it is a fundamental question because it involves an understanding of God and man. True self-identification is based on divine Principle. It is the spiritual fact of being.

Webster gives as one of the definitions of *identification*, "state of being identified," and of *identity*, "sameness with itself; self-sameness; oneness."

A most important word in the vocabulary of Christian Science is *one*. In the Christian Science textbook, *Science and Health with Key to the Scriptures* by Mary Baker Eddy, we read (p. 267): "God is one. The allness of Deity is His oneness. Generically man is one, and specifically man means all men." The oneness of God is His infinite self-containment, including within Himself His infinite idea or self-expression. All that is going on, then, is going on within the all-inclusive oneness of Mind. Thus Christian Science reveals Principle and its idea one, one Being; God and man one, one selfhood infinitely reflected or expressed within His own infinite self-containment.

Infinity is one continuous whole. It is individual because it is indivisible; hence God, Spirit, is the source and substance of all individuality, and individuality is as eternal as God. That which is infinite cannot be divided into parts, for parts would imply finity. There is no opposing element in infinity. In Principle there is nothing of a fragmentary nature. Continuity is an essential characteristic of God and man. Infinity is self-perpetuating, self-enfolding, self-sustaining, self-expressing. It has no opposite, no competitor, no boundary, no outside. It is without limit in power, capacity, and excellence.

God's revelation of Himself to Moses as "I AM" establishes, for all time, true identity. And obedience to the commandment, "Thou shalt not take the name of the Lord thy God in vain," (Ex. 20:7) disposes of mistaken or false identity, and forbids the association of "I am" with anything unlike God. Nothing which does not express God, Spirit, has or is identity. "I AM THAT I AM" is the effortless energy of infinite Mind, expressing and revealing itself as divine idea within its own measureless infinitude.

In Christian Science, God and man are one as infinite Principle and its infinite idea. Principle is absolute. Idea, likewise, is absolute. *Absolute*, according to Webster, means ". . . free from mixture; . . . free from limit; . . . free from the variability and error natural to human cognitions and perceptions; hence, actual; real." Principle expresses itself always as law. The law of divine Principle constitutes the divine idea and identifies it, and the idea partakes of the nature of Principle. Law, order, and perfection characterize whatever represents Principle. Mrs. Eddy writes in *Science and Health* (p. 475): "Man is idea, the image, of Love; he is not physique. He is the compound idea of God, including all right ideas; the generic term for all that reflects God's image and likeness; the conscious identity of being as found in Science, in which man is the reflection of God, or Mind, and therefore is eternal; that which has no separate mind from God; that which has not a single quality underived from Deity; that which possesses no life, intelligence, nor creative power of his own, but reflects spiritually all that belongs to his Maker."

The word *idea* comes from a Greek word meaning "to see." God's idea is, in fact, God's seeing or cognizance of Himself; it is the action of Mind knowing itself. Webster defines *idea* in part as "an embodiment of the essence of something." Thus man is the embodiment of the very essence of God. Essence, from the Latin *esse*, to be, is "that which makes a thing what it is; . . . prime or ultimate nature." Man is the spiritual embodiment, or reflection, of all those fundamental qualities which constitute the wholeness of God. He is God's infinite concept of Himself. Idea is as essential to Mind as Mind is to idea.

God, by reason of His very nature, is forever expressing Himself in action, unfoldment, development, and power. There is no element of mortality, of stoppage, obstruction, arrestment, passivity, stagnation, friction, loss, defeat, or exhaustion in Mind. Mind is perpetual action, the rhythm of being. Mind considering its own measureless content, Soul cognizing itself as glorified consciousness, Life perceiving itself in infinite manifestation constitute the infinite idea, or ideal man.

Supposition says that man—the reflection of infinite Spirit—began with physical conception, germination, development; that he is one of many, each with a separate mind, each incomplete and unsatisfied; each striving at the expense of another for self-expression and satisfaction. But this is not man. It is only a mortal misconception of man. Individuality and identity are spiritual, hence perfect; they do not change; they are never lost. Reflection is as permanent as God. Individuality and identity never were in matter nor of it. They never began; they never had to become; they simply are. In proportion as we realize this great spiritual fact of being, human limitations are self-extinguished and self-annihilated.

Studying the Concordances to Mrs. Eddy's writings, we find that reflection is expression, revelation, manifestation, identity. Reflection, or spiritual identity, seems transcendental to human sense simply because it so far transcends in glory, beauty, actuality, and completeness that which the physical senses can perceive. The substance of reflection is the spiritual oneness of effect with cause. The all-important point to remember is that reflection is Mind's contemplation of its own content. Reflection is complete in Mind; it never is outside of Mind, hence its permanence and continuity.

Every problem in human experience reduces itself to a belief of incompleteness. Poverty is incompleteness, the belief that supply is lacking; sickness, the belief that health is lacking; death, the belief that life has ceased or changed or departed. Sin in all its forms is the belief that man is incomplete, unsatisfied, and that because of his incompleteness he steals, lies, lusts, hates, and murders. Healing in Christian Science is the demonstration of Paul's statement, "Ye are complete in him"—Christ. Man is complete as the divine idea of God.

God's creation is always at the standpoint of perfection. In divine consciousness there is no imperfect concept; hence there is no incurable disease, no hopeless situation, no helpless mortal. Furthermore, because man reflects the infinite inclusion of Deity, he includes all ideas. He manifests the self-sufficiency of divine Mind. He includes the universe—the full expression of God. Self-sufficiency is the law of his being. Thus he does not have to get supply; he includes supply. Likewise does he include safety, home, health, satisfaction, peace, happiness, activity, usefulness, companionship, everything that goes to make up the completeness of being.

The truth of being, understood and utilized in Christian Science, appears humanly as the filling of the human need; in reality it is the action of Truth dispelling false belief with the revelation or manifestation of that which divinely is. In other words, it is our true spiritual self appearing. This appearing, though apprehended humanly in a form tangible to the physical senses, is wholly spiritual. This spiritual appearing is demonstration, and demonstration is divine! God is the law of perfection to His own idea, and when this is understood it is perceived humanly as a law of instant adjustment to every situation.

Identity, then, is not touched by any phase of the so-called mortal dream. It has never been conceived or brought forth in the flesh. It has never gone through the stages of infancy, growth, maturity, age, decay. Identity never dies. It is neither lost nor found through the mortal belief of death. Jesus referred to his spiritual identity as "the glory which I had with thee before the world was" (John 17:5). Man's identity, his individual conscious being, is one with the Father, intact in the foreverness of Life, the impregnable realm of reality. It is ageless, fadeless, deathless. It exists throughout eternity, for man is the conception of Life eternal. We know our identity in the measure that we know God. Identity, which is the spiritual sense of body, expresses the beauty of holiness, the agelessness of eternity, the symmetry of Principle, the purity of Soul, the continuity of Life, the perfection of being, the nature of divinity. It is the reflection of God. It is you as God sees you and knows you, and as Christian Science enables you to know yourself.

Then let our reply to the question, "Who am I?" be always, I am the infinite expression of infinite Being, of the one "I AM"! Mrs. Eddy says in her *Miscellaneous Writings* (p. 205), "The encumbering mortal molecules, called man, vanish as a dream; but man born of the great Forever, lives on, God-crowned and blest."

—*L. Ivimy Gwalter*

LOVE AND CHURCH RENEWAL

What can be said of coldness in the church, lack of caring, lack of spiritual affection?

Do we rejoice spontaneously over the warmth and love we find in our church body? Or do we have cause for sadness?

Our Leader, Mary Baker Eddy, was outspoken on this subject after addressing a communion service in The Mother Church in 1896. With compassionate realism she wrote to friends, "I find the general atmosphere of my church as cold and still as the marble floors." And she commented in another note: "My students are doing a great, good work and the meeting and the way it was conducted rejoices my heart. But O I did feel a coldness a lack of *inspiration* all through the dear hearts (not for me, Oh no, they are loyal to the highest degree) but it was a stillness a lack of spiritual energy and zeal I felt" (Robert Peel, *Mary Baker Eddy: The Years of Authority*, p. 97).

Throughout her years of founding her Cause, how patiently and fervently Mrs. Eddy stressed the vital necessity of Christian warmth and affection in the church—as well as in the heart of the individual worker! She emphasized that Christly love is indispensable to healing. As she writes in *Science and Health with Key to the Scriptures*: "The vital part, the heart and soul of Christian Science, is Love. Without this, the letter is but the dead body of Science,—pulseless, cold, inanimate" (p. 113).

Such words thunder Christ Jesus' teachings. In the Sermon on the Mount we find admonitions not to return evil for evil but to turn the other cheek, not to try to remove the mote from our brother's eye without casting the beam out of our own eye, not to come to the altar with a gift until we're reconciled with our brother. Our Way-shower counsels us to love our enemies and bless them that curse us (see Matt. 5–7).

This spiritual standard for all human relationships reverberates throughout the New Testament. In I John alone we find: "He that hateth his brother is in darkness"; "He that loveth not his brother abideth in death"; "He that loveth not

knoweth not God"; "If we love one another, God dwelleth in us, and his love is perfected in us"; "He that dwelleth in love dwelleth in God, and God in him" (2:11; 3:14; 4:8, 12, 16).

Metaphysically speaking, the true Church is a divine idea. It is made manifest to humanity, in a degree, not only as a necessary institution but also as the Christlike spirit—the inspired and spiritualized state of thinking—that animates the institution and is in fact the essence and substance of it. Even on the human level, however, we don't find our church just in buildings or organizational structure, but in the Christlike consciousness expressed and shared by the members. What counts is the healing elements of Love that prevail!

If we seek renewal in our church, then let there be a renewal of spiritual love.

If we want revival in our church, let there be a revival of invigorating Christian affection.

If we yearn for a feeling of freshness in our church, let there be an influx of kindliness and charity.

If we desire regenerated activity in our church, let there be increasing consideration for others and generosity of heart.

If we want a resurgence of healing power, let there be less destructive criticism and more gratitude and gentleness. More warmth of spirituality. Love is the source of all vitality. It sweeps away discord. Mrs. Eddy writes, "The way to extract error from mortal mind is to pour in truth through flood-tides of Love" (*Science and Health*, p. 201). Those "flood-tides" can sweep away the debilitating elements of mortal will, egotism, hurt, animosity, ill feeling, suspicion, undermining—and nothing else can.

Our need is to translate love as theory into love in action. Only by doing this can we lift our sense of organization from the ordinary human level, so filled with the collision of mortal traits, toward demonstration of Christ-impelled and spiritually governed relationships.

How can we do it?

Love means not just sporadic healing in our church, but spiritual love permeating the consciousness, aims, and atmosphere of the church so fully that the spirit of Christ-healing prevails in every service and every activity, as well as in the lives of individual members.

Love means honesty—not twisting facts to suit our purposes or saying one thing when we think the opposite. It would preclude thinking evil of another while outwardly professing good will.

Love means separating erroneous traits from our concept of the other fellow—through the method Science gives for correcting our own concept of God and man—then repudiating the error as nothing (unreal in God's all-presence) and maintaining our Christlike love for the one concerned. Love certainly means not spreading destructive criticism of fellow members (or others).

Love means patience and forbearance with one another—not reacting hotly. Forgiveness too.

If love is to prevail, cliquishness and attention to social status must give way to openhearted welcome and a feeling of brotherhood with those of other social, economic, and ethnic backgrounds.

One can meet such a requirement only by seeing with spiritual sense the spark of genuine Christliness in others.

Love means appreciating our fellow members and expressing this appreciation. A little caring, a little encouragement sincerely expressed, are like the widow's oil in the story of Elisha—these multiply without stint and enrich us all (see II Kings 4:1–7).

Love is the opposite of indifference toward our neighbor in trouble. A church that loves is a caring church.

Love means not letting detailed rules shut out magnanimity. The Christlike healing consciousness must not be chilled by formalism or ritual.

Translated into organizational relationships, Christian love must include those daily reflected graces of Spirit that warm the heart of both giver and receiver: courtesy, sensitivity to others, thoughtfulness, kindness.

To be specific, this would include making sure to tell committee members information they need to know for their work. It would include not taking arbitrary or secret decisions on matters that should be referred to the membership as the sovereign body under the governing rules. Courtesy

would also preclude a committee chairman or other member from deciding issues or taking action without consulting the committee itself; also, from countermanding an instruction given by another, even if one has the authority to do so, without telling the one who gave it.

Good communication is vital to good organization. And good communication springs from love.

Lacking such elements of brotherly consideration, an organization may tend to be harsh and restrictive. But learning the spiritual love that is kindly and considerate, true followers of the Science of Christ are pioneering a purified concept of organization that advances Christ's aims and blesses all—through its spirit even more than through its mechanisms.

Love calls for the moral courage to state one's position humbly and clearly, even though others may disagree and vote one down. It prompts us to abide willingly by legitimate decisions, trusting God to correct anything needing correction, even our own attitude, and to govern the church. Surely it means not holding grudges or letting them prompt our actions. It means wholeheartedly supporting what our branch church has decided by democratic vote to do.

In deciding church actions, love requires putting prayer *first*, before the administrative issues. Prayer means listening for Love's guidance, not just praying for one's own view to prevail. Otherwise, the dreary cycle of clashing opinions, mortal willfulness, and factionalism may gain momentum.

No material question relating to a physical building, for example, is more important than building trust and good will in the hearts of the members. Why? Because spiritual love is the divine consciousness made manifest; administrative choices are but human options, though subject to divine guidance.

Wouldn't love include turning to the Bible and our Leader's writings, not to find justification for one's own partisan view, but in humble listening to let Truth lead—with a readiness to change one's human opinion if necessary?

There's nothing wrong with organization per se, but a great deal that's right and necessary about it. When it's governed by spiritual motives and methods, it serves God's purpose, as our Leader teaches. When difficulties arise, what's at fault is the as yet undestroyed traits of mortal mind. But these can be controlled and purged through the Science of Truth and Love. As we let divine Love govern our own thoughts and actions in practical ways, what first appears as a trickle of love-filled aspirations can become a vigorous stream of spiritual momentum in church affairs.

Renewal in the church begins with ourselves—and with the irresistible power of God's ineffable love brought to light in demonstration.

—DeWitt John

THE OFFICE OF THE CHRIST

The revelation of Christian Science to this age is blessing not only each Christian Scientist, but indeed all mankind as well, through the redemptive work of healing which is going on daily and hourly. As Christian Science healing is understood, it is seen to be the coming of the Christ to human consciousness.

The office or function of the Christ is always to heal, or to restore harmony. In order to understand and appreciate Christ-healing it is necessary to know what the Christ is, and through the precious revelation of Christian Science the Christ is understandable to human consciousness. The many references on the subject found in the writings of Mary Baker Eddy show that the Christ is the Son of God, the divine image and likeness, the spiritual idea of divine Love. Would not this indicate that the Christ is the true identity of each one?

On page 333 of *Science and Health with Key to the Scriptures* are these words: "Abraham, Jacob, Moses, and the prophets caught glorious glimpses of the Messiah, or Christ, which baptized these seers in the divine nature, the essence of Love." As we realize the truth of our relationship to God, we are conscious of our spiritual selfhood, and this is the coming of the Christ to consciousness. Then we know ourselves as we are known of God, reflecting the divine nature, and we are indeed permeated with "the essence of Love."

Because Christ is an impartation of God and is inseparable from Him, as Jesus proved, the power and glory of Christ are God's. The Christ is and always has been the spiritual idea of divine Principle, and to claim any aspect of the Christ as a personal attribute or accomplishment is to misunderstand Christ. This false sense must necessarily be devoid of the healing power.

Because each case of Christian Science healing, no matter what the claim may be, involves the realization of the truth of God and His creation, what blesses individually as healing blesses also the whole human family. This may be seen from a statement contained in *Science and Health* where Mrs. Eddy says (p. 561), "To John, 'the bride' and 'the Lamb' represented the correlation of divine Principle and spiritual idea, God and His Christ, bringing harmony to earth." The word *earth* lifts thought to glimpse the scope of divine healing and shows the magnitude of the healing work. As we view the chaotic world conditions of today, what greater inspiration do we need to remain constant in our work as metaphysicians?

Christian Scientists use the word *healing* often in their thinking and conversation. As mankind in general accepts and appreciates what the word means in Christian Science, resistance to Truth will end and in its place will be an eager reaching out for divine healing. It is well for Christian Scientists also to ponder often the meaning of the word, for our work as metaphysicians is effective only as we understand the healing process.

Christian Science healing, or the bringing of harmony to earth spoken of by Mrs. Eddy, is the appearing of true identity to consciousness, which results in the complete eradication of the claims of error, whatever they may be, and the consequent restoration of harmony. This evidences divine perfection appearing right where the erroneous condition seemed to be, the holiness of man forever maintained by his heavenly Father being demonstrated here and now. Healing in Christian Science is seen to be the immunity from sin, sickness, and death which Truth and Love bring to us through realization of our sonship with God.

It is apparent that since the office of the Christ is to heal, the Christ and healing are inseparable and simultaneous. The appearing of Christ, Truth, to consciousness means the disappearing of error; the true idea of man annihilates the lie about him, and this is healing. Because the Christ is the essence of Love, it comes with all gentleness and tenderness to take away the illusions of the senses. It is resistless in its function. There is no question about darkness disappearing when the light is turned on; neither can there be any question as to what happens to error when the healing truth appears to consciousness. Where the error goes or how it disappears is of no more consequence to us than the question of what happens to the darkness. What we experience as time in the healing work is our spiritual maturing, our coming up to the point of complete realization of divine perfection.

The eternal harmony and perfection of spiritual creation is the forever fact. It is always in the present, or the eternal now. Much of the frustration and futility of human thinking stems from the fallacy that salvation must be an experience of the future, perhaps tomorrow, or at some vague future date, or even in that interminable, fearsomely mysterious experience called the hereafter. But God and His Christ are bringing harmony to earth, and freedom from mortal belief is a present possibility. Christian Science demonstration is in reality the claiming of divine perfection now.

In Revelation are recorded these illuminating words (11:15): "And the seventh angel sounded; and there were great voices in heaven, saying, The kingdoms of this world are become the kingdoms of our Lord, and of his Christ; and he shall reign for ever and ever." This clearly indicates that no group or nation is outside the realm of the Christ-power and that no nation or group is failing to feel its healing touch. Because the Christ is at one with God, who is ever present, healing is ever operative and is in reality going on everywhere. For this reason, every Christian Science treatment, although individual in its application and effect, touches all mankind and goes on in its healing efficacy to bring out the brotherhood of man.

The Christ can have no opposer in its healing office of redeeming mankind from the beliefs of the flesh. What is designated as the anti-Christ is the belief of carnality or hatred, but because there is in reality no power to propagate such a belief, no realm in which it can operate, no mass-controlled mentality to believe it, it can be proved to be completely without activity or manifestation. When the Christ is demonstrated fully by mankind as being at one with God and manifesting His power everywhere, all mortal belief will be utterly and wholly dispelled. Whether the error be called necromancy, mesmerism, hypnotism, animal magnetism, spiritualism, theosophy, sin, disease, or death, it will disappear. The Christ uncovers the illusive modes of mortal mind only to prove their nothingness.

The Christ-consciousness is entirely free from mortal illusion of any kind. It includes no false sense of sympathy with mortal mind's seeming dire effects, but annihilates the belief in its reality without effort and forever. The Christ is as unconscious of sin, disease, or death as is God. The purity of divine consciousness destroys every phase of mortality, and it is thus that we experience the healing touch of the Christ.

As we each become conscious of the presence of Christ, Truth, and thereby see the nothingness of evil and its claims, we are effectively helping to bring about the end of mankind's slavery. Our beloved Leader, in speaking of healing in *The First Church of Christ, Scientist, and Miscellany,* says (p. 253): "What nobler achievement, what greater glory can nerve your endeavor? Press on! My heart and hope are with you.

" 'Thou art not here for ease or pain,
  But manhood's glorious crown to gain.' "

—*Florence C. Southwell*

OUR FATHER'S DEMAND—UNSELF MORTALITY

*I*n the ninth chapter of John, the beloved disciple tells of the healing by Christ Jesus of a man who had been born blind and of the God-empowered spiritual idea Jesus used to accomplish the healing.

The man was a beggar, sitting by the way where Jesus came. Observing him, Jesus' disciples asked, "Master, who did sin, this man, or his parents, that he was born blind?"

Jesus bypassed the question the disciples asked as to what had caused the beggar to be blind. Instead he declared, "Neither hath this man sinned, nor his parents: but that the works of God should be made manifest in him" (John 9:2, 3). Was not Jesus affirming the great spiritual, eternal fact that the true selfhood of this mortal existed only "that the works of God should be made manifest in him"? From God Jesus knew that indestructible sight is always the gift of eternal, all-seeing Mind to its continuing emanation, man.

To have his faith in God's healing power evidenced, Jesus bade the blind man go and wash in the nearby pool of Siloam. He did so, and came seeing.

The claim of the evil, mortal mind, that it had made, physically embodied, and hopelessly afflicted this mortal was proved untrue, without substance. The enduring intactness of man, whose status is always to evidence the works of God, one of which is permanent perception, was demonstrated.

Jesus thought as his Father Mind caused him ever to think. He recognized the eternal, spiritual truth that man's only cause is the eternal God, good, and man is God's perpetual effect. This God-given and God-empowered realization of man's permanent, perfect, spiritual nature nullified, in an impressive degree, the lying suggestions of evil that there is a dominant, destructive, material cause, and compelled mortal mind to govern its body harmoniously, not afflictively.

Such truth-empowered thinking restored the mortal's entire organism of physical sight and caused it to function normally. Thus his human sight was restored by the Word of God, right when and right where mortals ignorantly believed it had been destroyed.

This illustrates the teaching of the Discoverer and Founder of Christian Science on the subject of belief in sensible matter. Mary Baker Eddy writes, "We should subjugate it as Jesus did, by a dominant understanding of Spirit" (*Unity of Good*, p. 50).

In the textbook, *Science and Health with Key to the Scriptures*, among what Mrs. Eddy calls the chief stones in the temple of Christian Science, she lists first the postulate "that Life is God, good, and not evil" (p. 288). Nothing can be closer to any of us than Life. To know God is our only and forever Life, we must spiritually cognize our indissoluble and continuous oneness with Love, God, which it is God's function ever to have us do.

Mrs. Eddy confirms and commands: "Life is eternal. We should find this out, and begin the demonstration thereof" (*ibid.*, p. 246).

To find Life, Jesus thus defined the way: "And this is life eternal, that they might know thee the only true God, and Jesus Christ, whom thou hast sent" (John 17:3).

Not many years ago I felt an inward impulse to more actively deny, challenge, and reject, every day, the mortal sense of life, and faithfully to open my thought to find more of man's one real Life, God. I was confident this could be done through prayer.

At first there was some mental hesitation and reluctance to initiate the effort. But I knew my leading was from the Father and must be obeyed. Soon the work became unlabored, joyous, rewarding. Legions of angels silently whispered the thoughts God was providing to enable me to fulfill His command to love Him, my only Life, more, and to surrender any lingering belief I had in a self separated from God.

An angel thought from the textbook said, "Man in Science is neither young nor old" (*Science and Health*, p. 244). What is man, then? I asked. The answer was, "As timeless as the Life that is my forever God."

This helped me confidently to reject the

suggestions of the material mind that I was an old mortal, getting older. I asked, "Just what says that?" I recognized it was the one liar, mortal mind, talking only to its counterfeit, mortal concept of man. I affirmed that the "I" that is factually "I," mortal mind cannot know. It is eternal Mind's self-expression, forever of and in Mind's infinitude.

Jesus' saying reassured me, "No man knoweth the Son, but the Father" (Matt. 11:27). That I accepted as logical. How can anything but man's forever source know what man forever is?

In the many revelations of God's Word in the Bible, I recognized, God is communicating exactly what is the ever-continuing status of man, God's own emanation and likeness.

My purpose, I saw, was not to add a few years of mortality to my human experience. It was to align my thoughts more fully with my omnipresent, omniactive God, my forever Life and immortality.

Here let me divert a little to say something about this concept we call time, which aggressively claims it has a stranglehold on life and makes man to be first young and then old, and predestined to die.

Years ago I was impressed by the thought, which I found in a well-reasoned article in *The Christian Science Journal*, that time is merely the measurement of the movement of matter bodies. Our earth, one body of matter, revolves around a fixed sun, another body of matter, and we conclude that a year has passed. The body of matter called the moon revolves around the earth and we say a month of time has gone by. The earth rotates on its own axis and we say a day of time has passed. Then human thought irrationally concludes that this oft-repeated movement of ignorant, unthinking matter bodies in some unexplainable way becomes a law of destruction or impairment for mortals. It makes thinking mortals old and eventually converts them into a heap of dust.

An optometrist usually asks his patient, whose sight he would improve, "How old are you?" He has been falsely educated to believe that time is the conditioning force of the patient's sight. He does not know that the only cause of man is his intelligent, creative Mind, which forever provides permanent perceptivity for its witness, man.

In a complete reversal of this ignorant buildup

of time, Mrs. Eddy states: "Never record ages. Chronological data are no part of the vast forever" (*Science and Health*, p. 246). She meant this. It is an indispensable step toward timeless Life and out of mortality.

Also, Mrs. Eddy reminds us that man is never a statistically defined mortal. He does not originate from a material sperm and evolve into a fleshly body, calling for a birth certificate and scheduled, not many years after, to end with a death certificate—perhaps with a man-ordered or man-numbered social security card, or its equivalent, in between.

In my work I became more sure than ever before that Mrs. Eddy spoke as the messenger of God, our ever-continuing Life. I realized that better healing must come from a fuller understanding of man's forever and permanent oneness—unity—with God, his everlasting Life.

Why not demand of ourselves now to initiate the mental effort indispensable to dispose, step by step, of the totality of godless mortality? What is mortality? Who knows? Our Leader did. She says, "…sin is mortality's self, because it kills itself" (*ibid.*, p. 468). She could so simply define sin as mortality's self because she discerned so clearly that sin alone hides immortality.

Even a satisfying glimpse of the eternal fact that man's only Life is now God brings with it a more secure and satisfying sense of existence. What Mrs. Eddy calls the friction of false selfhood (see *Miscellaneous Writings*, p. 104) lessens the heavy mental baggage of conflicting personalities, and their opinions fade before the dawn of the simple fact in our consciousness that God, being the only Life of all, is the one infinite Person, forever making all and uniting all in Love's one grand symphony.

Our Leader, Mrs. Eddy, teaches, "The great spiritual fact must be brought out that man *is*, not *shall be*, perfect and immortal." Then she gives specific instructions as to the first step we must take to do this. She declares, "We must hold forever the consciousness of existence, and sooner or later, through Christ and Christian Science, we must master sin and death" (*Science and Health*, p. 428).

I am convinced it is not difficult to do this if one really desires to do so. Is it not divinely natural continuously to think the thoughts that cause one to blend with his forever Life, his alone source?

In the divinely ordered consciousness of man there is inevitably a perpetual sequence of right ideas causing him to coincide with the unlabored motion of God's government of His all-inclusive kingdom.

The only alternative to forever holding the consciousness of existence is to surrender one's sense of selfhood to the fiction of material life, called mortality, wherein sin, disease, death, and dust are the only pattern of being. Accepting this fatalistic concept of existence, one becomes the slave and victim of the time trap of mortality.

The choice is for you and me to make. There is no sidestepping Life's demand if we are factually to live.

A very serious barrier to progress in understanding God as our alone Life is procrastination, putting off until tomorrow what we can at least start doing today. This is a common barrier to worthy progress of many kinds. Individual awakening—deep, genuine, persistent—must come to nullify this futile lie of ignorant delay.

Often I have noticed in the thought of many Christian Scientists a shyness and unwillingness to initiate, and continue, the mental effort indispensable to finding and feeling the ever-present, spiritual facts of Life, always as near as thought.

Something about the word *must*. It is not in the [written] Concordances to Mrs. Eddy's writings, perhaps because of its grammatical classification as an auxiliary verb. But she uses it over three hundred and fifty times. She uses it to define precisely what we can do to dispose of mortality. Here are some of her words: "Mortals must drink sufficiently of the cup of their Lord and Master to unself mortality and to destroy its erroneous claims" (*The First Church of Christ, Scientist, and Miscellany*, p. 161). That is exactly what the Way-shower did; he unselfed mortality. He accomplished this liberation from the entirety of mortality in a comparatively few years. And exactly the same forces that he used are provided by the one Father for each of us to use.

He did not wait for the crowd. He knew his salvation was between himself and his Maker. So is ours. What is the degree of our willingness to think of our one Father as our only present and eternal Life? That is the question.

Many Christian Scientists are daily, in some degree, unselfing mortality, but all of us are capable of doing much more.

All members of The Mother Church accept this tenet of Christian Science given in the textbook: "And we solemnly promise to watch, and pray for that Mind to be in us which was also in Christ Jesus; to do unto others as we would have them do unto us; and to be merciful, just, and pure" (*Science and Health*, p. 497).

It was this Mind that was in Christ Jesus that healed the blind man of blindness and liberated the Master from mortality. More humble willingness to accept this Mind as the only Mind and Life there is for each of us is what is so sorely needed to help us more fully to fulfill our promise.

In conclusion, I saw that our Way-shower by his enduring example, and our great Leader by sharing the potent activity of God's revealed Word, were saying that the inescapable demand on each one of us is to align our thoughts, moment by moment, more completely with our heavenly Father and His angels, presently—because eternally—just at hand to enable us to unself mortality.

The accomplishment of this demand may be a long-continuing one, but let us remember we cannot find any objective to compare with this one, and the rewards are immediate and continuous. What can mean more to an individual than to know he is on the straight and narrow way to eternal Life? And our Leader assures us, "The way is narrow at first, but it expands as we walk in it" (*Miscellany*, p. 202.).

The sum of it all is that in the exact proportion we are willing, individually, to accept God as our forever Life, we unself mortality.

—*Paul Stark Seeley*

THE PASSING OF THE SEA GULL

*T*wo women sat upon the deck of an ocean liner in that sweetly satisfying silence which only true friends can understand. One of them had recently experienced what seemed to be the supreme tragedy of her life in the passing from her sight of a loved one, and there was still an ache in her heart which her friend had been endeavoring to assuage by tender, comforting assurances regarding Life and immortality. The one who had been listening sat quietly, her hands folded, trying to grasp what had just been said, and at the same time idly watching the sea gulls play about the mast as the ship plowed its way over the dancing waters. Presently she noticed that one of the gulls had left the others, circling ever higher and higher, until it was evident that it had separated itself from them altogether and was taking a course straight away from the ship. On and on it flew, steadily, surely, its strong white wings outspread, until it became but a mere speck in the sky and finally was lost sight of altogether.

But has the sea gull gone anywhere? thought the silent watcher, who was still pondering those comforting words she had just heard of the teaching of Christian Science regarding what is called death. Had that beautiful activity ceased? Was it not still identified with life, and strength, and vigor, and all that it possessed when it passed from her view? Had anything stopped? She suddenly sat up in her chair and gazed in almost startled interest at the blue far horizon, as into her consciousness there flowed an indescribable peace, the first she had known in many weary months. For she saw the truth of what her friend had been telling her and realized as never before that what had happened in her experience was just like the passing of the sea gull beyond her range of vision: it was still going on and on, even though her limited, human sense of sight could no longer follow it.

If I could see only a little farther, she thought. And that is exactly what Christian Science enables us to do—to see a little farther, or, in other words, to discern more clearly something of the great realities of being hidden to mortal sense. As one gains a greater understanding of Truth, as given in the Christian Science textbook, *Science and Health with Key to the Scriptures* by Mary Baker Eddy (the

Discoverer and Founder of Christian Science), he finds that his spiritual vision becomes enlarged as he grows each day into a better understanding of God and of man's relationship to Him. As he continues to study and ponder this simple, practical, new-old religion—new as each morning with its fresh opportunities, as old as the Galilean hills among which Christ Jesus walked and taught—he finds that there is in it not only healing for the sick and reformation for the sinner, but comfort for the sorrowing. He sees that although his sea gull may not turn back in its onward flight, its going has lost its sting, and the words of Isaiah are once more marvelously fulfilled, "He hath sent me to bind up the brokenhearted, . . . to appoint unto them that mourn in Zion, to give unto them beauty for ashes, the oil of joy for mourning, the garment of praise for the spirit of heaviness" (Isa. 61:1, 3).

As one casts aside the cold mantle of sorrow in which he has enwrapped himself, and steps out into the warm sunshine of Truth, he finds that his experience has made his loved one not less dear to him, but, rather, more dear, because he has learned something of that universal divine love which does not confine itself to those who first love us, but holds all humanity in its embrace. He no longer cries out in the dark for the "touch of a vanished hand," but reaches out his own to comfort and bless those others along life's highway whose path for the moment is dark, too, and to tell them of the peace which is for all of God's children, the peace which the world can never give or take away. Thus he proves the truth of what is written in *Science and Health*: "The wintry blasts of earth may uproot the flowers of affection, and scatter them to the winds; but this severance of fleshly ties serves to unite thought more closely to God, for Love supports the struggling heart until it ceases to sigh over the world and begins to unfold its wings for heaven" (p. 57).

Let us ever think aright about those who have passed beyond that blue horizon. They are in reality completely identified with that divine Life which knows no end because it knows no beginning. Let us never think of them as associated with anything else, but say in our hearts what the Shunammite woman of long ago said when questioned by Elisha's servant about her son, whom the world called dead; for in response to the question, "Is it well with the child?" she answered, "It is well" (II Kings 4:26).

—Louise Wheatley Cook Hovnanian

"THE PATTERN OF THE MOUNT"

Through the revelation that came to Mary Baker Eddy there has been vouchsafed to Christian Scientists spiritual understanding of the Master's teachings with attendant power to obey his commands to heal sickness and sin and to break the hold of death. Insofar as they remain true to this trust they are servants of mankind and leaders of nations. They are cities set on hills of thought, where demonstrations of Christian healing may be seen by all men. No prophet of old was provided with greater authority and power from on high than is the consecrated Christian Scientist of today. And no Christian Scientist has less obligation of devotion to this bestowal than did the ancient men of God to their earth missions.

The healing work of Christian Science patterns the Biblical records of divine deliverance of men from evil, because it emanates from the same source that inspired prophet and apostle. It is functioning today to warn humanity of enemy errors, to guard the gates of thought, to strengthen the walls of courage, and to cause the reign of righteousness to appear in more permanent aspect. In mental watchtowers of the world it heralds the presence of the peace of God.

To experience greater evidences of divine healing power in all the walks of life today is doubtless the desire of many peoples. Christian Scientists are humbly and earnestly striving towards this goal in their dealings with themselves and with their fellow men. They have learned in some degree that such healing occurs through the energy of holiness recognized and yielded to by human consciousness. And they have found that the effects of this energy become more apparent as thought turns from the contemplation of materialism and abides with spiritual reality. In proportion as men turn unreservedly and continuously to God for help in every situation, divine healing appears as more than an occasional occurrence; it becomes uninterrupted evidence of omnipresent, supreme harmony. It is the command of the Christ, not the demand of mortality. Inspired analysis of Christ Jesus' example reveals the essence of his healing efficacy and indicates how men today may successfully follow the method of their elder brother.

What Jesus knew of his spiritual background contributed vitally to his healing work. Every individual has a spiritual background. The Master knew that man is always the son of God, the offspring of Spirit, dwelling in the eternal Mind. When confronted with sense testimony to the contrary, he remained at the standpoint of spiritual realization. What he humanly did at a moment of healing was of secondary importance. His abiding with what he had always known and lived of spiritual being was the essential factor. His preparation of divine consciousness equipped him to deliver men from false beliefs. Not what he learned about the human situation, but what was always real to him in eternal existence, was his effectual asset.

From this height of holy consciousness the Master met and overcame every mortal testimony. His consciousness never yielded to the presentations of evil. Leprosy, prenatal disfigurement, hypocrisy, injustice, hunger, murder, mortal so-called law, and death gave way before the spiritual understanding of man as the son of God. Jesus did not start to overcome error when it presented itself to him. So far as he was concerned it was always nonexistent, because he knew man's pre-existence and eternal being as the perfect offspring of God.

Mrs. Eddy writes in her textbook, *Science and Health with Key to the Scriptures* (p. 427), "Immortal Mind, governing all, must be acknowledged as supreme in the physical realm, so-called, as well as in the spiritual." This is just what Jesus did. He ever knew the spiritual fact to be reigning, not struggling with mortality. The physical realm, so-called, is but the false sense of existence, and so is no realm at all. Jesus never knew the power of immortal Mind as battling with the flesh when it touched the suppositional realm of physicality. He never thought in terms of divine power attempting to establish its kingdom in the midst of opposition. He knew that wherever God is, He is All-in-all, and that God is everywhere.

When truly acknowledging immortal Mind, Spirit, Principle, as supreme in the physical realm, so-called, human consciousness ceases to be aware of physique, disease, personal sense, evil. It is freed from the mesmerism of belief of life in matter, of struggle against evil, and is established in the peace and dominion of spiritual understanding. Diseased sensation is no longer recognized as information about the condition of man's being, and divine consciousness is accepted as the truthteller. This is the way whereby seeming bondage to the flesh is ended, the way whereby our Master reached final resurrection and ascension.

Divine healing is a coming up to the mount of revelation; a purifying as though by fire; an irresistible uplifting of consciousness to behold the presence of "the body of heaven in his clearness" (Ex. 24:10), the spiritual identity of man. It was on the mount of revelation and transfiguration that man's eternality and divinity appeared as concrete being to Peter and James and John. They suddenly became aware of, and then temporarily lost sight of, that which was continually apparent to Christ Jesus. Jesus never descended from the height of spiritual perception where the ideas of God are tangible reality. The mount of revelation becomes the mount of transfiguration as divine healing occurs.

In Exodus we read that when Aaron and the children of Israel saw Moses after his experience on Mount Sinai "the skin of his face shone" (34:30); and in Matthew we read that on the mount of transfiguration Jesus' "face did shine as the sun" (17:2). The three disciples saw and heard Jesus and Moses and Elias talking together. The mortal sense about these men was silenced, and the eternal facts concerning them became vividly apparent. No one was seen to be held in matter, to be subject to age or death, or to be absent. The individual identity of each one was recognized as divine and eternal.

On the mount of revelation and transfiguration, in other words at the moment of divine healing, thought is divorced from human doctrine, creed, therapy, experiment, and fear. It is consciously at one with divine reality and law. It is able to see the handiwork of Spirit. It can hear the voice of God declaring man to be His beloved son. Thought ceases to be the slave and victim of material sense and experiences the liberty of divine reality. The shapes of matter vanish, and the forms of Spirit become visible. The words of St. Paul that both body and spirit are God's become manifest to uplifted thought.

A little child stands naturally on the mount of divine healing, eager, responsive, receptive, unafraid. The adult sometimes has to climb there over the obstacles of self-opinion, false education, or mental resistance. But the transfiguration from God's hand awaits them both. In her *Message to The Mother Church for 1901* Mrs. Eddy writes (p. 10), "Divine Love spans the dark passage of sin, disease, and death with Christ's righteousness,—the atonement of Christ, whereby good destroys evil,—and the

victory over self, sin, disease, and death, is won after the pattern of the mount."

"The pattern of the mount," of divine healing, as we see it in this experience of Jesus', is not one of human argument, but of wordless beholding. The pattern is one of divine dominion, not one of personal contention; one of human stillness before the presence of omnipotence. It is a model of spiritual daring, rather than of priestly conservatism. This manner of healing requires self-immolation, purity, innocence, and sacrifice. It is a wholly spiritual way which disdains human acclaim, worldly power, and personal emolument. It is devoid of weakness, asceticism, and timidity. "The pattern of the mount" is one of spiritual nobility, before which every bastard belief of mortality flees. It is the pattern for the practice of all Christian healing.

When the ten lepers were made whole, Jesus was on the mount able to show them somewhat of their true identity. When he raised Jairus' daughter and when he was in the tomb, he was on the mount of transfiguration, revealing to human consciousness the eternal man of God's creating. Only on the mount of revelation does transfiguration occur, does mortality yield to immortality, does the evidence of eternal Life and perfect identity appear. Only at the height of spiritual cognition do we lose sight of mortal self and know man as he is known of God. Divine healing is the transfiguration experience, the climax of the revelation to human consciousness of man's preexistence and eternal identity as the son of God.

And where is the mount of revelation and transfiguration? In its metaphysical meaning it is more than a landmark of Palestine, more than a regional location where a never-to-be-repeated miracle occurred. This mount is wherever human consciousness sheds its sandals of mortal belief and knows that it stands on holy ground. Jesus knew the presence of the mount in the halls of government, beside the country roads, and in the synagogues. Peter, Paul, and John were aware of its presence in prison and in exile. Mrs. Eddy found it among the New England hills. It stands through all the past and looms on the horizon of the future. Only those who ascend the mount in the company of the Christ, the true idea of God delivering men to the uttermost, behold the heavenly vision. On the mount of revelation and transfiguration surely all things are possible with God.

Spiritual healing is Christ's requirement that all

Christians practice what they preach, be what they profess, do what they acclaim, become humanly humble and spiritually mighty. It is the measuring rod of religious attainment which plumbs the depth of Christian sincerity. This subject is one so deep and broad and high that human sense cannot yet compass its measure. The Christ-work penetrates all space and knowledge with power of resurrection from every materialistic belief. It is more than world-wide; it is thought-wide.

About this subject Mrs. Eddy writes pungently (*Miscellaneous Writings*, p. 174): "Let us have a clearing up of abstractions. Let us come into the presence of Him who removeth all iniquities, and healeth all our diseases. Let us attach our sense of Science to what touches the religious sentiment within man. Let us open our affections to the Principle that moves all in harmony,—from the falling of a sparrow to the rolling of a world. Above Arcturus and his sons, broader than the solar system and higher than the atmosphere of our planet, is the Science of mental healing."

The Master included only three of his disciples in his experience on the mount of transfiguration. Today Christ, Truth, is lifting multitudes to the height of divine perception and transformation. Divine healing occurs in the spiritual altitude and attitude where communion with God unfolds into concrete being. This occurrence requires no setting within religious ceremony; rather does it indicate escape from ritual. No suppositional skill of the human mind in medicine, surgery, or mental manipulation could possibly initiate it. Only as human consciousness rises above the level of mortal belief does it behold the wonders wrought by the hand of God. Divine healing accomplished in any age is the fulfillment of divine law and prophecy to men.

Wherever the power of divine deliverance touches the world today it unites the hearts of men, reveals the presence of the order of heaven, establishes justice, and opens possibilities of research and discovery beyond the so-called realm of matter. Its overcoming of disease, though far-reaching in its scope, is yet the least part of its capability, for it has come to exchange the whole material concept of existence in human thought for the spiritual reality of the universe and man. Such appreciation of the term *divine healing* takes it far afield to meet the needs of nations as well as of individuals in the provinces of physics, economics, government, education, and religion, as well as medicine. It is the most potent factor for good there is in the world, because it is the power of God with men, revealed again in Christian Science according to "the pattern of the mount."

—*Julia M. Johnston*

PERCEPTION

A physical scientist has stated that the human eye perceives but one forty-thousand-millionth part of the material universe. How inadequate, then, is this physical organ as a medium for reliable information! By far the greater part of what is taking place in the temporary so-called material universe the eye never sees; and it takes no note at all of the permanent spiritual universe of divine Mind. Says Paul, "Eye hath not seen, nor ear heard . . . the things which God hath prepared for them that love him" (I Cor. 2:9). Where, then, is that perceptive capacity to be found that acquaints us with God and His work?

Christian Science turns back the testimony of matter, denying that either man himself or the senses of the true man are in matter, and affirming that the true man and his senses are the expression of eternal Mind and endowed with the permanency of divine Mind. The important fact is often overlooked that there must be Mind in order to have sensibility. "Mind alone possesses all faculties, perception, and comprehension," writes Mrs. Eddy in the Christian Science textbook, *Science and Health with Key to the Scriptures* (p. 488). Without Mind there can be no perceptive sense. Perceiving is a mode of Mind's activity.

God is referred to by Mrs. Eddy as the "all-seeing" (*ibid.*, p. 587). Where is the seeing activity of God taking place? That is like asking, Where is the Life that is God expressed? or, Where is the Love that is God made evident? God, Mind, has one and only one mode of expression, namely, His ideas. The true individuality of each one of us is God's idea, and as such must express the perceptive activity of the all-seeing Ego. This perceptive activity of God, just as the knowing and loving activity of God, is eternally operating in, is evidenced by, and is inseparable from, His ideas.

This discovery leads to important conclusions. Man's true perception is the individualized expression of God's seeing, just as man's living is the individualized expression of God's living. Since man's sight is an individual mode of God's seeing, his sight is as substantial and continuous as is God's seeing. The permanency of divine Mind and all its faculties is conferred on its idea. We must therefore gain an understanding of man as God's idea.

In the divine order there can no more be impaired sight than there can be impaired Mind, a depleted intelligence, or a blinded God. True perception can no more be impaired than God's activity can be interrupted, or the perpetual omniaction of Mind can be abrogated or lessened. If one idea could lose its perceptive faculties, or have them impaired, such result would evidence a power greater than the all-seeing Mind. God would no longer be all-seeing. Loss of perception would isolate the idea from those relationships and associations which characterize the divinely coordinated unity of Mind's ideas, and the perpetual indivisibility of God and His universe.

The perceptive faculties afford the ability to discern the identity of each and all of Mind's ideas. Impairment of these faculties, if such were possible, would disrupt the unity and intelligent association of God's ideas in one universal family. In the eternal continuity of perceptive activity, expressed by God's ideas, is evidenced the omniaction of the all-seeing Mind.

What argues against these conclusions? Material thoughts and physical sensation. How much credence is to be accorded such testimony? None. Why? Because it is a denial of the divinely intelligent standard of life and manhood, and is therefore a negation, a lie.

The lie asserts there is another mind, the opposite of God, good. It claims that this mind evolves matter and resides in matter. It admits that there must be mind in order to have sensibility, but it says: I am mind, and I am in matter. Therefore, it argues, sensibility is in matter; sight and hearing are material. Where is the fallacy? Just here: that mortal mind is devoid of intelligence, the essential quality of Mind; hence it is never Mind. To call it mind is a contradiction in language, as Mrs. Eddy states in her textbook (p. 114). Mind is never mortal. Because it is never Mind, so-called mortal mind never has sensibility. Never having sensibility, it cannot endow a mindless, substanceless organism with faculties which it does not possess.

What seems to be impaired vision is a changing deflection of error's lie that mind and sensibility are in organic matter. Difficulties arise when we believe we are what mortal mind says we are,—its very own, created and conditioned by and dependent on matter and material sense,—instead of realizing that we are what God, divine Mind, knows we are, even His eternal, unimpaired and unimpairable idea, seeing as He gives us to see, not by or through matter, but in spite of it. Our conscious associations with one another and with creation are forever preserved to us by reason of God's ability to sustain Himself and His own all-seeing ability. All the being we have, including our seeing, is in Him and is His. The infinite One's eternal consciousness of His infinite selfhood includes the perceptive faculties of every idea.

The belief, then, in impaired vision, which sometimes inflates itself into a popular contagion, is due primarily to the misconception that mind is in matter, and that perception is therefore in matter and suffers destruction or impairment, which are the conditions always consequent to mortal thinking. When it is understood that Mind is not in matter, it becomes apparent that sensibility cannot be there. The lie of defective sight must then disappear, for there is nothing to support it.

Though mortal mind, hiding behind its effect, claims that the eye sees, Science shows that it does not. So-called mortal mind alone believes it sees material things, even as it alone believes it cognizes mortal thoughts. When mortal mind abandons the body of its making, the eye does not see, though its organic structure is unchanged. As true perception is gained, the temporary objects—mortal thoughts, the objects of material sensibility—gradually give place to the permanent ideas of Mind, which afford evidence and proof that God is.

When mortal mind finds an auditor for its plea of impaired sight, it presses its lie with persistent aggressiveness. Perception is constantly needed to maintain contact with men, books, and things. Under the guise of necessity, corporeal sense would try to force concession, retrogression, and a prolongation of its claim that matter first gives sight, then takes it away, and then demands material appendages in order for man to continue to see. Sometimes it would bolster its arguments by comparison. It reminds us that a friend, perhaps a practitioner, is wearing glasses. For us to do so would not be so bad, it whispers! Thus it plies its deceitful way. Personal comparison is more likely to leave one at the unavailing shrine of human personality than to advance one Godward. Man's one obligation is to be man—to represent, which means to express, the all-seeing Mind. What mortals do, or do not seem to do, cannot change what man must do. If the use of temporary means to aid human vision seems to some the lesser of two evils for the moment, let it be remembered that such means can

be only temporary. The individual should never be content until such means have given way to that perfect perception bestowed of God. To give the lie of impaired perception a continuing place in one's mental home is to shelter a denial of God's nature.

True perception is gained as we gain the Mind of Christ, the divine consciousness which knows that God is All-in-all. Because he possessed this spiritual-mindedness in some measure, Jacob was able to perceive the angels, ideas of God, in their harmonious heavenly activity. It was this consciousness which enabled Daniel and John to discern the apocalyptic visions, so indicative of the substantiality of things unseen by physical sense. The transfiguration showed the ability of true perception to see beyond the clouds of earth-sense and find conscious association with Moses and Elias, despite many centuries of time, thus evidencing the indivisibility of God's family.

Not good eyes, but good thoughts, are the medium of true perception. The former result if the latter are entertained. Since perception is a faculty of, and is inherent in, divine Mind, we are conscious of it only in the degree we are at-one with the divine Mind. We are consciously at-one with the divine Mind only as our thoughts are that Mind's thoughts. Consciousness must become consciously Godlike, must express love, goodness, unselfishness, purity, honesty, spirituality. While criticism, condemnation, hatred, dishonesty, selfishness, sin, fear, abide in thought, how can divine perception be known? No one of these is seen of God, and it is His seeing that is expressed by man. Three times our beloved Leader questions us in the opening lines of the Communion Hymn (*Poems*, p. 75). Each question has to do with perception:

"Saw ye my Saviour? Heard ye the
   glad sound?
 Felt ye the power of the Word?"

The three succeeding lines point the way which, if followed, will enable us to answer aright.

"'Twas the Truth that made us free,
 And was found by you and me
 In the life and the love of our Lord."

—*Paul Stark Seeley*

POSSESSION

❦

*T*here is a belief among mortals that they can become the privileged possessors or owners of something. When through the usual process of law a man acquires real estate, he has a strong desire to erect a fence around it and to keep everybody else away. Then follows the belief which is universally acknowledged, that he owns a certain amount of the earth's surface and that the law protects and defends him in private possession thereof. He builds a house and occupies it, calls it his own, and no one is permitted to approach or to enter it contrary to the owner's wishes without being considered a trespasser. In our present degree of development it is generally understood that property is something which *should* have an owner; that the earth and all that is contained therein may be divided into parts and parcels, and that different individuals may claim possession of more or less of it to the exclusion of others. All this, however, is based on the supposition that matter is substance and that man is the proprietor of it.

Through the illusive processes of mortal belief truth is apparently reversed; thoughts are externalized into things, and these things are claimed, held, and dominated by individuals. Some people have a large amount of property, others a little, while a great many have none at all. This apparently unequal distribution of material possessions fosters envy, jealousy, and strife, often provoking the one who finds himself deprived of his heart's desire into the use of questionable means, if not of physical force, to gain his object. It would be safe to say that nine tenths of all the war and contention in the world has been inaugurated and carried on because of the invasion of so-called property rights, or because of a desire to extend material possession or dominion.

Just as soon as a man finds himself in possession of a certain amount of matter,—of houses or lands, of stocks or bonds,—he is besieged by a sense of personal responsibility for his wealth and a fear that he may at some time be dispossessed of it. The whole system of property rights and of the division of property is based upon the supposed substantiality of matter, an illusion which some day must be dispelled by the law of God, which declares that Mind is the only substance. This change may not be brought about all at once, but through right thinking and conduct there will in due time be established the true concept, namely, that

"the earth is the Lord's, and the fulness thereof" (Ps. 24:1). Rightfully speaking, everything in this world belongs to God, and through reflection belongs also to man who is the image and likeness of God. When we have reached the point in our demonstration where we can resolve things into thoughts, the multiplication of these thoughts will be possible, so that every individual may reflect and possess all that belongs to his Maker.

In some lines of thought this ideal condition already prevails; for example, in mathematics. Let us suppose that the figures used in making calculations, instead of being accepted as thoughts, were regarded as material objects. In such a case every mathematician or accountant would have to provide himself with a supply of figures, which would perhaps be made of some durable material like wood or iron, and which he would keep on a shelf or locked in a drawer. When the mathematician wished to use the figures he would take them out, arrange them in their proper order, and be enabled thereby to work out his problems.

If in a busy season the accountant's supply of figures should become exhausted, he would have to purchase more or perhaps borrow them from his neighbor. He might approach a fellow worker and say, "I wish you would lend me two or three fives and a few sevens this morning; I am out of these figures." His friend might reply, "I am sorry, but I have been using so many fives and sevens lately in my work that I need all I have and cannot accommodate you." There might even be a shortage in figures which would affect the whole population, and there would be a scramble for a supply. The price of figures would advance, and if people really believed that these objects were a necessity, there would be such brisk competition that the price of enough figures to do business with would be out of all proportion to the cost of their production, and many people would have to do without them.

This condition of affairs, however, is impossible because of the fact that figures instead of being *things* are *thoughts*, and as such are everywhere present without limit or restriction. No contrivance of mortal mind nor any scheme of manipulators can take away from us one single figure or deprive us of instantaneous access to all that we can possibly have use for. No war has ever been declared because one nation has attempted to appropriate more than its share of the multiplication table, nor has any man been found guilty of using figures which he has surreptitiously taken from his neighbor.

Figures are not things but thoughts; they are mental concepts, and as such they are available to everybody. Sometime it will be realized that not only is this true with regard to figures, but that every so-called material object in the universe is but the counterfeit of some divine idea and not what mortal mind represents it to be. The time will come when mortal mind will abandon its belief that ideas are represented by material objects, and when this time arrives there will be no fear of loss of, or damage to, that which we understand to be an idea and not a thing. We shall then be able to realize what Jesus meant when he said, "Lay not up for yourselves treasures upon earth, where moth and rust doth corrupt, and where thieves break through and steal: but lay up for yourselves treasures [right ideas] in heaven, where neither moth nor rust doth corrupt, and where thieves do not break through nor steal" (Matt. 6:19, 20).

You may ask what all this has to do with our present demonstration. A great deal. Christian Scientists may add to their peace of mind and freedom from responsibility by thinking along right lines and endeavoring to put into immediate practice the teachings of Christian Science. If a man is engaged in a business which he believes to be his own, of which he thinks he is the creator and proprietor, and for the success of which he deems himself personally responsible, there may be a great sense of burden attaching to his position. He may suffer from poor business, loss of trade, or any of the beliefs which go with his particular occupation or profession; so long as he feels that the business belongs exclusively to him, he will never be free from some of the countless beliefs that are supposed to affect trade in general and his occupation in particular. The remedy for this condition is for the man to begin to declare and to know that all is Mind and Mind's ideas; that there is nothing whatever about his business that is limited or material. If God is the creator of all, and if everything in the universe belongs to Him, then this business which the man calls his own is really God's, and the man becomes the master of it only to the degree that he conforms his thoughts and his daily transactions to the Sermon on the Mount. If he recognizes this, and applies his understanding of the Principle of Christian Science to his work, his fear and uncertainty will vanish. He will find himself conducting and carrying on business in the manner God requires it to be done, and he will exercise dominion and control over it just to the extent that he places himself under the unerring direction of divine Mind.

If a woman considers herself the owner of a home and that everything in it is hers; if she believes she has furniture and fixtures which are her personal property as well as every other household accessory, she may become so burdened with responsibility as to find herself utterly inadequate to control the situation. But if she is willing to accept God as the ruler of her household, to convert things into thoughts and to understand that "all things were made by him; and without him was not any thing made that was made" (John 1:3); if she can realize that divine intelligence governs and controls her servants, her house and everything that is contained therein, she will immediately lose all sense of care, fear, and confusion, and find that the divine law of peace and harmony has taken possession of her household and manages it. If she realizes that everything about the house is designed to bring out and express the law of perfection, things will run much more smoothly for all connected with this establishment, and peace and joy will come to all who enter therein.

There is another phase of possession which is perhaps one of the strongest of mortal beliefs. Parents believe they are the privileged creators of something; that they can usurp the creative power of divine Mind and have children of their own, for whose bringing up, education, and future welfare they are entirely responsible. This feeling on the part of parents opens the door wide to the suggestion of failure, and the trials and tribulations which are supposed to go with the ownership and control of children assail them from every side. They must learn that God is the only Father and the only Mother; that man is the offspring of God; that he is not physical and material, but spiritual, reflecting and expressing the wisdom, love, and intelligence of infinite being. As soon as this line of thought is touched upon, the false sense of responsibility which mortal mind has placed upon parents is taken away, and they can then in the right way trust God to take care of their children, knowing that nothing can interfere with the harmonious results which accompany divine protection.

All belongs to God; nothing belongs to us. Man is neither a creator nor an owner. As Christian Scientists we can begin the realization of this at once, and the results will be speedy and satisfactory. But when we relinquish all thought of personal possession, this does not mean that we must sacrifice everything we hold dear or that we shall really be deprived of anything. On the contrary, it means that through an increased understanding that all is Mind and the ideas of Mind we shall gradually come into possession of all that is worthwhile. The mere act of surrendering something is not in itself a virtue, nor is there anything to be gained by assuming a false sense of humility. It is true that there is much to give up, but it is always the old, unsatisfactory beliefs which we are parting with, and as these disappear they are supplanted by right ideas, which give to us a greater sense of freedom, power, and possession than we ever had before.

What did Jesus mean by the statement, "…he that hath, to him shall be given: and he that hath not, from him shall be taken even that which he hath" (Mark 4:25)? Why, this: that the one who possesses the right idea is really the one that "hath," and his possessions are bound to increase; while the one who has the wrong thought is the one that "hath not," and he must of necessity lose even that which he seems to have. What we need to do, then, is to change our method of thinking. Jesus' saying, "…seek ye first the kingdom of God, and his righteousness; and all these things shall be added unto you" (Matt. 6:33), is made possible only through Christian Science.

Mary Baker Eddy, the Discoverer and Founder of Christian Science, says, "Holding the *right* idea of man in my mind, I can improve my own, and other people's individuality, health, and morals;…" (*Miscellaneous Writings*, p. 62). All things are accomplished through the right idea, which asserts itself in human consciousness and dispossesses us of our false beliefs. The only thing that can happen to the human sense of things is that it disappears in exactly the proportion that we apprehend the truth.

It is a law of metaphysics that thought externalizes itself. Mrs. Eddy says in *Science and Health with Key to the Scriptures*, "Hold thought steadfastly to the enduring, the good, and the true, and you will bring these into your experience proportionably to their occupancy of your thoughts" (p. 261). From this it is apparent that the right idea in Christian Science naturally expands into expression and brings thought into a demonstration. When we attain the standpoint from which we can see all material things as beliefs only, and that these beliefs can be transformed and improved through holding the right idea, we shall then begin to bring into our experience the things referred to by Paul when he said, "…Eye hath not seen, nor ear heard, neither have entered into the heart of man, the things which God hath prepared for them that love him" (I Cor. 2:9).

Another line of thought which suggests itself at this juncture, is that mortals believe they are in possession of a mind apart from God which they call their own, and that they can think and will as they please with this mind, regardless of the facts of being. This belief leads to another erroneous conclusion, namely, that mortal mind has created and placed us in possession of a corporeal body including eyes, ears, lungs, stomach, etc., all which we believe to be material, and for the well-being of which we are responsible. When this error takes possession of us, the next thing that mortal mind claims is the ability to deprive us of sight, hearing, etc., and that our stomach can become disordered or diseased. This is all the result of believing in another creator besides God, another intelligence and power to which we yield obedience. "Know ye not," Paul says, "that to whom ye yield yourselves servants to obey, his servants ye are to whom ye obey…" (Rom. 6:16). The only remedy for the ills of the flesh is to correct the false beliefs that produce them by introducing the right idea. It is the failure to see this that sometimes prevents Christian Scientists from doing the quick healing of which they are capable. In the textbook, *Science and Health*, the author says: "By not perceiving vital metaphysical points, not seeing how mortal mind affects the body,—acting beneficially or injuriously on the health, as well as on the morals and the happiness of mortals,—we are misled in our conclusions and methods. We throw the mental influence on the wrong side, thereby actually injuring those whom we mean to bless" (p. 397).

In mortal mind's method of thinking, thoughts become externalized as matter and are called the body. When we understand what Christian Science teaches in regard to the externalization of thought, we shall see that the human concept of bodies is a mental product and is nothing more or less than the outward expression of thought. Therefore, to heal what seems to be a diseased condition of the body, we must drop all thought of the body as being material and recognize it as a purely mental product, an objectified condition of material sense, the correction of which, by replacing the false belief with the spiritual idea, will according to the law of God produce health and harmony.

God is the only creator, and all that He creates must be like Himself. Man is not composed of flesh, blood, bone, and nerve; on the contrary he is the individualized aggregation of right ideas, the compound idea of God which includes these right ideas. "For God to know, is to be;…," Mrs. Eddy says (*No and Yes*, p. 16).

Knowing is being; therefore what man knows constitutes his being, and true consciousness consists in the reflection of those right ideas which already exist in the divine Mind. It is scientifically impossible to put a wrong thought into consciousness, and there can be no imperfection in Mind, since whatever is included in Mind is perfect and inviolable and can never be changed or altered in any way. Nothing exists but God and what God creates, consequently there is from the lowest to the highest only one right idea of anything, since "the divine Mind maintains all identities, from a blade of grass to a star, as distinct and eternal" (*Science and Health*, p. 70), as the textbook says.

Mortal belief in its endeavor to see materially creates the human eye and declares it to be the organ of sight, while in reality sight is a quality of Mind, and is entirely independent of iris, pupil, lens, or other parts comprising the visual organism. When Jesus said, "The light of the body is the eye" (Matt. 6:22), he was not referring to a material sense of eye, but to that mental or spiritual discernment which divine Mind bestows upon man. We must remember, however, that man is not a material object, he is mental; that is to say, he is the image and likeness of Mind, the embodiment, expression, or reflection of ideas only. That there is such a thing as perfect eyes—spiritual discernment—there can be no doubt. It is equally true that every spiritual faculty which divine Mind includes is bestowed upon Mind's image or reflection, man. A knowledge of this would restore to perfect health a diseased condition of eyes, as well as it would restore what is called the lost substance of lungs. Note what Mrs. Eddy says in *Science and Health:* "The indestructible faculties of Spirit exist without the conditions of matter and also without the false beliefs of a so-called material existence" (p. 162). That quality of divine intelligence which is back of what is called the human eye, and of which the human eye is but the counterfeit, is the only eye there really is.

This is also true in regard to what mortal mind calls heart, liver, lungs, and all else that go to make up the so-called material body. Mortal mind claims that man is organized matter, but mortal mind's beliefs are not substantive, and the fact remains that the only man there is or ever can be is that compound spiritual idea of which this material organism is the counterfeit. Inasmuch as there can be only one right idea of everything, there is only one right concept of what mortal mind calls stomach. It is not made of matter; it is not a material thing. It is a mental concept or a thought, the substance of which is in Mind. A material concept of any of the physical organs is false and misleading, and must eventually be destroyed. "Every object in material thought will be destroyed, but the spiritual idea, whose substance is in Mind, is eternal," says Mrs. Eddy (*ibid.*, p. 267). And elsewhere she asks, "But, say you, is a stone spiritual? To erring material sense, No! but to unerring spiritual sense, it is a small manifestation of Mind, a type of spiritual substance, 'the substance of things hoped for'" (*Miscellaneous Writings*, p. 27).

It is time for Christian Scientists to stop trying to doctor sick organs and devote themselves to exchanging their imperfect models for better and higher ideals, which is the only true method of healing. God is the law of health and harmony to all His own ideas, and not only is this true, but the law of God which governs the perfect spiritual idea is also the law of perfection to the human belief of things and this extends to every organ of the human system. What God knows about hand, eye, foot, is all there is to know about them. He knows them not as material, but as perfect, harmonious, and useful ideas, and that their identity is distinct and eternal. If a man has the wrong concept of hand, eye, foot, his only salvation is to exchange the objects of sense for the ideas of Soul. These ideas are perfectly real and tangible and are within the reach of all who turn to divine Mind for guidance. If one's body should be injured, it would be his belief or concept of body that is affected, not God's idea, and the remedy is for him quickly to give up his erroneous belief of body and acquaint himself with God's incorporeal idea. "Acquaint now thyself with him [God], and be at peace," the Bible says (Job 22:21).

In *The First Church of Christ, Scientist, and Miscellany* Mrs. Eddy writes: "Neither the Old nor the New Testament furnishes reasons or examples for the destruction of the human body, but for its restoration to life and health as the scientific proof of 'God with us.' The power and prerogative of Truth are to destroy all disease and to raise the dead—even the self-same Lazarus. The *spiritual* body, the incorporeal idea, came with the *ascension*" (p. 218).

We can have no other body than the one perfect incorporeal idea. Man being the compound idea of God, it naturally follows that everything which is included in the consciousness of man must be spiritual and perfect, or it is not the consciousness that God knows and which man must have. Matter can never be spiritualized; but our mistaken belief which presents itself as matter must be corrected and thus spiritualized. To heal an imperfect heart, which is simply a wrong belief, one must repudiate the testimony of material sense and claim the presence of God's idea, in order to improve his false concept. It is not necessary that he should know just what the spiritual idea back of the human belief of heart is. All he needs to know is that his mistaken sense of heart, which appears to be material, is not the right one. There is a divine idea of which the human belief of heart is the counterfeit, and that idea is present now and here, and there is no other. As stated in the textbook, "When examined in the light of divine Science, mortals present more than is detected upon the surface, since inverted thoughts and erroneous beliefs must be counterfeits of Truth" (*Science and Health*, p. 267). If a man has an unhealthy belief of stomach, the only remedy is to recognize the falsity of all that mortal mind says about stomach and claim possession of the divine idea, which is the only perfect reality.

All sickness is due to a wrong belief of things, and the only remedy is to get the right idea. Because every spiritual idea is counterfeited by a material belief, we can understand what Mrs. Eddy means when she says, "Divine Science, rising above physical theories, excludes matter, resolves things into thoughts, and replaces the objects of material sense with spiritual ideas" (*ibid.*, p. 123). If there were no spiritual ideas with which to replace objects of material sense, our diseased beliefs could never be corrected and our bodies could not be scientifically healed. God is not separate from His ideas; the spiritual idea of anything is always present and carries with it the power and activity of infinite Mind, and when this spiritual idea is brought to bear upon the false belief, it produces a harmonious result.

If it is true that a wrong belief concerning body manifests itself as a disordered material condition, then the right idea which corrects the false belief must produce an improved physical manifestation. We can never heal by attempting to exercise the power of Truth on a sick body. It is the exercise of the power of Truth on a *belief* of sickness that produces the healing results.

Christian Science is an exact science, and as such it will permit of no deviation from its Principle and rule. It demands that the student, in order to demonstrate its truth, must be able to meet its requirements. Jesus said, "...ye shall know the truth, and the truth shall make you free" (John 8:32). Therefore a knowledge of the truth of what Christian Science teaches is absolutely necessary to its demonstration.

We are all laboring more or less under the belief that man is a human being separated from his creator, with a mind and an intelligence all his own. This belief must be destroyed, and the only way to accomplish its destruction is by constantly holding in thought the right idea and by declaring the presence and activity of all the ideas of God. As these ideas become more real to us the so-called human mind will disappear and we shall find ourselves growing more like Him,—more like infinite wisdom, more like Truth and Love. Then it shall come to pass as is written by the prophet, "...the earth shall be full of the knowledge of the Lord, as the waters cover the sea" (Isa. 11:9).

—*Adam H. Dickey*

THE PROBLEM OF THE HICKORY TREE

A certain hickory tree which shades our lawn has lately been the means of teaching so valuable a lesson that its story is here told for the benefit of others who, figuratively speaking, may have hickory trees on their own premises.

Each year when the arrival of spring causes the other trees to put forth their leaves, this one stands for weeks in gaunt and bare unloveliness. The sun may shine its brightest, the soft winds may blow, the warm summer showers may beat as they will, but there is no response; while all around is growing green and beautiful, it alone remains coldly aloof, taking no part and apparently wishing to have no share in the general awakening. Yet we are never concerned about it, for we know that after a while tiny buds will appear, which will swell and grow without unfolding until they stand all over its gnarled branches like stiff little Christmas candles. Then perhaps there comes a night of rain followed by a day of brilliant sunshine, and lo, a miracle is wrought! The Christmas candles soften and uncurl into baby leaves, which hang for a few days like feathery tassels, and then imperceptibly assume such shape and color that, almost before we are aware, our stubborn old hickory tree stands clothed in a garment of green which is a delight all the season long.

Once, as we were enjoying its luxuriant shade, the thought came, Why can we not be just as patient with our loved ones who are having their struggle in getting started, as we are with trees? People, as well as trees, have characteristics of their own, and is there any occasion to fret and worry because all mental processes are not alike? The violet pushes through the wet leaves at almost the first breath of springtime, while the rose requires weeks of care and vigilance on the part of the gardener before it reaches its full splendor. Yet who can say that one is more lovely than the other? Is the violet in any position to criticize the rose, or should the rose judge and condemn the violet? Each is simply unfolding after its own nature, and neither self-righteousness on the part of the violet, nor self-condemnation on the part of the rose, will facilitate the growth of either. Then shall we have less patience with our brother and our sister than we have with the grass of the field, "which today is, and tomorrow is cast into the oven" (Matt. 6:30)?

Suppose we look back and honestly ask ourselves if we have always used the same simple common sense in our dealings with people that we used in regard to our hickory tree. As we passed back and forth beneath its bare branches, did it ever occur to us, for instance, to upbraid it for its slowness, or to stop and inquire why it did not begin to get green like the other trees? I am quite certain that we never shed tears over it, nor did we nag at it, and make its life miserable by continually begging it to put out a few leaves—"just to please us!" Neither did we call its attention to the weeping willow next door, and remark how happy those people must be with a fine tree like that in their yard. We just went quietly along, like reasonable people, attending to our own affairs, and feeling sure that the hickory tree was doing the same. Because it grew in our yard and belonged to us was no reason why it should lose its individuality, nor its absolute freedom to work out its own salvation in its own way.

Mrs. Eddy has reminded us of the need to "remember that the world is wide; that there are a thousand million different human wills, opinions, ambitions, tastes, and loves; that each person has a different history, constitution, culture, character from all the rest; that human life, is the work, the play, the ceaseless action and reaction upon each other of these different atoms" (*Miscellaneous Writings*, p. 224). Then why grow discouraged? Because no evidence of a change is visible to the material senses does not mean that it may not already be taking place in human consciousness. No one saw the inward struggle through which the tree had to pass before the hard bark softened sufficiently to let the first bud appear; and in like manner no one sees the conflict through which some natures grope their way toward the light. The heart's innermost processes are not always revealed, even to those nearest and dearest, but in this trying interval of waiting can we not have sufficient faith in the ultimate outcome to be a little more patient, a little more loving?

Perhaps, however, the argument comes, "It is my very love which makes me impatient. If I did not love so much I should not care." But is it really love, O troubled heart? Let us be sure on this point, for no sentiment is so likely to be misconstrued. If we probe the heart deeply enough, that which we fondly believe to be love for the tree sometimes turns out to be only love for ourselves,—a desire that the tree shall grow green because it will make our yard prettier, and in consequence we shall be happier. Before we begin to pity ourselves too industriously, and sadly maintain that we have done "everything we can," suppose we ask ourselves if we have done the one thing which is the hardest to do of all—so hard, in fact, that some of us never even attempt it—and that is, to let go of our own sense of personal responsibility in the matter.

Suppose we try a little harder to remember that it is not "our" tree at all, but God's. Suppose we try to make its stubbornness, its ugliness, its perversity, less of a reality, and to remember instead that the real tree and the real man are perfect ideas in Mind, and that, as such, God is ever conscious of them. Suppose we try to remember that God's work is already done; that the hickory tree, to Him, is already as beautiful as the weeping willow, because He can see that which is still hidden from our dull eyes—the perfect, finished spiritual creation; and that in His way (not ours) and in His time (not ours) this eternal fact will be made manifest to human consciousness.

Meanwhile do we honestly desire to see it work out its problem? Then suppose we step aside and give it a chance. It is possible that the one thing it needs is just to be let alone, and it is more than probable that this is the one thing which we have never done, for mortal mind is never more agreeably employed than when attempting to manage other people's affairs. Suppose we stand aside just for awhile. Self-righteousness may have been casting a darker, colder shadow upon it than we have ever realized. Self-love, too, which Mrs. Eddy tells us is "more opaque than a solid body" (*Science and Health*, p. 242), has sometimes kept the light from reaching things far more precious than hickory trees. The human mind has also a strange trait called self-justification; but, if we pray earnestly enough, we can free ourselves even from this. Do not let us crowd the slowly unfolding idea, for overanxiety has a smothering effect at times. Let us get ourselves far enough in the background to allow the free winds of heaven to blow and the warm sunshine to do its work. It was God's tree before it was ours. Can we not trust Him to take care of it?

Take courage, wistful gardener! Have weeks and months gone by, and still your tree stands without response? It may be that tomorrow's dawn will see the first faint bud appear; and in the mean time there is yet one thing which we can do, one final test so crucial that only those who have borne it can understand what it involves. Do we really love? Have we really the best interests of the loved one at heart? Then prove it. That which is truly love, and not its counterfeit, can not only

Speak the word that's needed, yet
Can hold its peace as well; nor doth forget
When things seem wrong, love shows itself
    most great
By sometimes being willing just to wait.

—*Louise Knight Wheatley*

A RECOMPENSE OF PROFIT

*J*esus' parable of the talents indicates that there is no essential difference between one, two, and five talents. They designate variety, not quantity. According to Christian Science there is but one quantity—the essence of the universal substance of Spirit, God, from which all qualities or attributes emanate. Talents are illustrative of the multifarious aspects of God. Thus one talent is as precious and as important as five talents to the infinite intelligence and so to the world.

Is not the underlying purpose of the parable to set forth the impartiality of God in a partial concept of creation and the equality of man's potential regardless of the scope of one's human operation? Is not the one-talent individual in reality as capable and as competent as the two- or five-talented ones, with respect to opportunity and achievement and productivity? The divine demand is that one's talents be employed. A recompense of profit will not accrue to the indolent.

Jesus believed in the just reward of industry, in individual responsibility to produce, to multiply and replenish the earth, to gain and possess and dispose. He taught that to him that has exercised his talents well shall be given a recompense of reward. And the inevitable recompense of loss is to him that refuses to employ his talent. And he taught and proved that as Mary Baker Eddy, the Discoverer and Founder of Christian Science, states it (*Science and Health with Key to the Scriptures*, p. 199), "The devotion of thought to an honest achievement makes the achievement possible."

There can be no insurmountable obstacle to the utilization of one's talent, and the use of it cannot fail to bring profit. Intelligent activity in any right field of endeavor is necessary to assure security, abundance, peace, contentment, all of which are the reward of unselfed service. One must employ his talent uninhibited by misgivings, doubts, and fears in order to reap the recompense of the divine profit system. And it is true that there is profit to be had even from mistakes if they are repented of and not repeated.

The real Christian Scientist faces only profit and no loss. How shall we conduct ourselves, then, in a social order tending progressively away from the individualism of Christianity as Jesus taught and lived it? He gave the example in this as in all other aspects of human life. When some Pharisees brought him a penny, he asked (Mark 12:16), "Whose is this image and superscription?"

"Cæsar's," was the reply.

Then Jesus answered, "Render to Cæsar the things that are Cæsar's, and to God the things that are God's"; and he paid his taxes and otherwise obeyed the laws of the land.

The Master took no active part in politics, and he made it clear to Pilate that his kingdom was not a worldly one. Mrs. Eddy once gave this statement to the press (*The First Church of Christ, Scientist, and Miscellany*, p. 276): "I am asked, 'What are your politics?' I have none, in reality, other than to help support a righteous government; to love God supremely, and my neighbor as myself." She was outspoken in her views and convictions, yet she always adhered to her divinely given mission and ministry. She used her talent and earned five more in fulfilling her destiny under the divine profit system of operative Christian Science.

In the application of divine Science to humanity there is no such thing as a nonprofit activity. Those fields white unto harvest, when reaped, pay off some thirty, some sixty, some an hundredfold.

There is nothing wrong with the universal Mind, God. There is nothing wrong with the spiritual idea, man, God's begotten Son, in whatever variation thereof. Health, perfection, all good qualities or ideas, belong to Mind and are the components of man. They are common to individual man, the man expressed in infinite variety or originality.

Mrs. Eddy, who viewed each mortal from an impersonal standpoint, did not see a mortal as spiritual. Rather, she sought to see the real person where a mortal appeared to human sense to be. In reality God is not over there in space and we over here. There is but one consciousness, Mind, individualized in man, as idea. And this real man is right where the mortal seems to be.

There are not two men, the real and the unreal. In the human consciousness there is the wheat, or true ideas, the reverse of the tares, or false conceptions. Whatever is good in human consciousness is real idea, is of God, and depicts the real man, and to see this good is to see by that much the real selfhood. Whatever is bad in human consciousness is unreal and on its way out, and to see it as bad is to speed its departure.

When the last tare is detected and destroyed the real man will be revealed in and as the right idea, man—the wheat. Thus we observe that all is profit in this husbandry, even the loss is gain. We see that the individual we now identify by name retains all the good characteristics or identity without the tares, or false concepts, which have now disappeared.

In the spiritual regeneration there will be no loss of identities, but there will be a retention and a glorification of all the good we have known in the individuals we have known and known of. There is never a loss of good. The vengeance of the Lord is upon evil, never upon good. The retention of good is as certain as the existence of good. Is not the Lord's way equal? Once one has found good to be a component of his being, he can never let it go; it is his consciousness, his being, his Life.

In the profit system of Christian Science we find a basic law laid down by the Master, "The labourer is worthy of his hire" (Luke 10:7). This presupposes honest devotion and endeavor, not the whine of a lazy lout. It means all that the honorable and glorious word *labor* means. It means what our Leader means when she counsels students to make an adequate charge for their services and then conscientiously earn it. It means what Paul meant when he pointed out that one who sows sparingly reaps sparingly; whereas one who sows bountifully reaps abundantly.

And Jesus expressed it thus: "Give, and it shall be given unto you; good measure, pressed down, and shaken together, and running over, shall men give into your bosom. For with the same measure that ye mete withal it shall be measured to you again" (Luke 6:38).

God will indeed come with a recompense of justice and of profit. Man in Science is the servant of Mind, of restful Mind. If our heart is in the job, what our hands have found to do, we can safely leave reward to the divine order, for giving and getting are one, and the one is giving. Service is the rationale of being, and he who serves not, litters the earth. In unselfed service one gains not merely merit but the dignity of the worthiness of his reward.

Although Jesus asserted that the poor are always with us, he in no way endorsed poverty or set his approval on it. He merely commented on a fact. But his whole life was affluent. It was this divine affluence which caused Paul to exclaim in awe and wonderment (Rom. 11:33), "O the depth of the riches both of the wisdom and knowledge of God!"

Isaiah perceived the wealth and wisdom of ideas and saw them enrich and ennoble barren lives. He perceived the divine recompense of close communion with Mind. He wrote (Isa. 48:17), "Thus saith the Lord, thy Redeemer, the Holy One of Israel; I am the Lord thy God which teacheth thee to profit, which leadeth thee by the way that thou shouldest go."

And does not our individual experience teach us that God's ways are profitable? The wealth of the Father is the riches of the Son. Like the widow's cruse, sources and resources never fail. Supply is the reflection of substance, and reflection is simply the objectification of thought. Money can be taken away from men, but they cannot be deprived of the constructive, the creative thinking which enables them to make money. That is why we say, "You can't keep a good man down." Always he has the recompense of profit.

If material riches can be piled up successfully, how much more can a recompense of ideas be acquired by the truly studious man who seeks always to be taught of God, Mind, to profit. It is so right to profit! The prodigal son by his folly experienced deprivation, but he learned to profit by his sharp experiences. He learned that it is folly to be wise in worldly ways and that the Father's kingdom is always attainable to us by walking in the only way to wealth, health, holiness, security, the way to the many-mansioned house of Mind's creation. He always wins who sides with God.

—*John M. Tutt*

REFLECTION

The subject of reflection sometimes presents a difficulty to the young student of Christian Science in that the often-used illustration of a mirror may suggest separation between that which is reflected and the reflection.

One definition, however, which Webster gives of the verb *reflect* is "to consider mentally, specifically, to attend earnestly to what passes within the mind; to attend to the facts or phenomena of consciousness." And *reflection* is defined in part as "any state in which the mind considers its own content."

On page 515 of *Science and Health with Key to the Scriptures*, Mary Baker Eddy writes, "The eternal Elohim includes the forever universe." The eternal Elohim, or infinite Mind, is self-contained, self-existent, self-expressed. God, being Mind, includes "the forever universe" as idea. There is but one Mind and but one universe. Nothing exists outside the realm of all-inclusive infinity.

Thus reflection is the action of Mind unfolding itself within itself. This unfoldment or revelation is spiritual creation. Reflection is never outside of Mind. It goes on always within Mind. It partakes of the nature of Mind, and expresses and utilizes the infinite capacity of Mind. It is wholly mental; and because Mind is Spirit, it is wholly spiritual.

Now how may we relate this concept of reflection to the illustration of the mirror? Every attempt to picture the divine or the spiritual in terms of the human, holds a discrepancy. No human illustration can perfectly portray the divine, but we may from certain figures and similes derive valuable lessons and food for thought. Thus Jesus taught the profound truths of the kingdom of heaven in parables of the leaven and the hidden treasure; and Mrs. Eddy uses the mirror to illustrate in some measure the function of reflection. She says in *Science and Health* (p. 515), "Call the mirror divine Science, and call man the reflection;" and in *No and Yes* (p. 9) she defines Science as "the atmosphere of God."

When we read about the mirror, let us think of the all-inclusive, all-comprehending Mind, or God, and man the reflection, appearing in full glory within that Mind, in the radiant atmosphere of Soul, himself the very evidence of the eternal oneness of divine being. Then we may "note how true, according to Christian Science, is the reflection to its original," even as Mrs. Eddy says in continuation of the above-referred-to quotation from the textbook.

Infinity is presence, coexistence, at-one-ment, incapable of separation. Thus reflection exists forever without time in eternity. It is instantaneous, unfluctuating, permanent, complete. It cannot be intercepted, interrupted, or mutilated. Reflection is action, not stagnation; unfoldment, not arrestment. The reflection which results from Mind's activity manifests both intelligence and substance. Delusion and depletion are unknown to Mind.

Reflection does nothing of itself; possesses nothing of itself; originates nothing of itself; is nothing of itself. Mind creates, animates, controls, governs, and constitutes its own reflection. God is cause; man is effect. Through spiritual sense, Mind cognizes itself in the infinitude of divine reflection. The reflection of infinite Mind is infinite.

Spiritual law sustains reflection. Reflection cannot be inverted. Therefore, there is no law, that is, no necessity, reality, or presence back of age, illness, death, or limitation, inasmuch as these do not exist within the infinitude of perfect Mind. Man is not a mortal, separated from God, vainly trying to reflect Him. Man is reflection. He is wholly spiritual. We should awake to this great spiritual fact of being, and demonstrate the possibilities it implies.

The true concept of reflection is the solution of the problem of lack. Humanity's continual effort is to multiply good materially. Human endeavor along the lines of research and accomplishment generally is directed toward this goal. Mankind labors for it, fights for it, sacrifices for it, even dies for it, but is never satisfied. From its very inception mortal existence is limitation; birth implies death, and everything in the mortal's experience between those two points is limited. Which of us has not at some time in his experience thought, If only I had more money, more health, more opportunity, or more companionship, my problem would be solved! But would it be? That which calls itself human, holds no solution within itself. Christian Science alone reveals the scientific, spiritual solution of the problem of being. The multiplication or increase of good is found in spiritual reflection alone. Man existing at the standpoint of infinite reflection knows no limit. The limits of mortal existence disappear in the demonstration of spiritual being.

Infinite reflection is abundance, not accumulation. It is expression, not hoarding. There are no vacuums, no waste places, no burdensome responsibilities, no dwarfing relationships in reflection. Each idea is distinct and free, governed by unerring divine Principle, moving, unfolding, progressing in accord with Principle. Reflection does not age, mature, or deteriorate. It never makes a mistake. It never dies. Reflection is changeless; it exists forever at the standpoint of perfection. It is unlabored, effortless, spontaneous, continuous.

The action of reflection never leaves a vacuum. Fear and limited material thinking produce the appearance of a vacuum—as, for example, of something made less by use. In the infinitude of spiritual reflection there is no vacuum. If it were not for fear and limited thinking, any appearance of a vacuum would be filled naturally and inevitably. Reflection cannot be diminished, obstructed, obliterated, or erased. It never stagnates. If Mind should cease to operate, reflection would cease to be. Spiritual consciousness is the demonstration of spiritual integrity. It fulfills its obligations. It is founded on divine Principle, and admits of no wantonness, wastefulness, or extravagance.

Likewise, when a loved one seems to pass from our sight, the all-knowing, all-loving, eternal Mind holds within itself the continuity, action, identity, and individuality of spiritual reflection without change, or lapse, or vacuum.

Infinite Mind supports its own spiritual creation. Supply is often thought of as personal support. We frequently hear it said, I have to support my home, myself, my family, and so on. And with that belief come fear, false responsibility, burden, limitation. Divine Mind, not human effort, is that which supports! Support, therefore, is wholly spiritual; hence limitless, actual, permanent, complete. It is as easy and effortless for the ocean to support the fifty-thousand-ton steamer as the tiny sailing craft. The sustaining power of divine Love, Spirit, is unlabored and unlimited.

The law of God is the law of abundance. Man in the likeness of God expresses abundance—the abundance of Spirit, of Love, of Life; therefore, abundance is natural to man. Christ Jesus said, "I am come that they might have life, and that they might have it more abundantly" (John 10:10). The barrel of meal and the cruse of oil may be the human concept of Love's provision in time of seeming famine, but Science demands that we progress beyond the belief of famine. The children of Israel were sustained in the wilderness, but their demonstration led them beyond the wilderness into the promised land. Within the allness of infinity, there exists neither famine, fowler, pestilence, nor wilderness. Infinite Mind, cognizing itself in spiritual reflection, is conscious of nought but its own infinitude.

Paul struck the keynote of scientific demonstration when he said, "Ye are complete in him"—Christ, Truth (Col. 2:10). Man in God's likeness is whole, secure, complete, and safe. He exists in God and reflects infinity.

—L. Ivimy Gwalter

RIGHT WHEN— RIGHT THEN

*B*ecause God eternally is infinite good, there has never been an instant when any phase of evil has been able to get a foothold within this infinity. The forever universality of God's kingdom, wherein all manifestations of God safely dwell, is uninvadable. Evil, ever suppositional and false, has no capacity to relate itself to God or to aught that is of and in Him. Evil's every thought, condition, or sense of selfhood remains forever outside God's allness—in falsity's nothingness.

In these simple verities are the answers to the many-faced lies of evil which so persistently suggest that somehow it has, in the past, broken through the gate to God's infinity and found a toe hold there. From such a suppositional beginning, it argues it has built a formidable case against one's life with which now to harass one.

But evil, the lying material mind, can do nothing but lie. It knows no truth to tell. When it repetitiously says that in the past it has caused, embodied, and adversely affected what it terms our material history, its every statement is a falsity. There is not a scintilla of evidence to support its claim, save its own never-to-be-believed material sense testimony. Lying evil tells its lies to its own suppositional states of thought and blindly believes it has proved its case when it says its lie is true.

"The true theory of the universe, including man, is not in material history but in spiritual development," writes Mary Baker Eddy, the Discoverer and Founder of Christian Science, on page 547 of *Science and Health with Key to the Scriptures*, the textbook of this Science.

Evil's number one lie is that it is a creative cause and has created you and me, through the processes of material parentage, to be mortals. Here, it says, is the beginning of our material history. Christian Science teaches one to answer:

"Right when you say you were cause to me, you lie; for right then God, Spirit, Mind, was my one and only parent, the eternally continuing source of all that is I.

"Furthermore, right when you say I was being formed materially, right then I was existing as the spiritual, everlasting, individual manifestation of the one, causative Mind. As Christ Jesus put it, 'Before Abraham was, I am' (John 8:58). So say I to you, lying evil, before material generation ever seemed to material thought to be, my Christly, Godlike selfhood was already divinely conceived, coexisting with the eternal Ego, which it lives to express."

Right when mortal mind may say laws of material inheritance were operating to condition one, right then Christian Science proclaims man's only selfhood as inheriting, deriving from his ever-continuing cause, all the faculties, qualities, abilities that are eternally native to his sonship with his Maker, the Father Mind. The Preacher saw the spiritual and eternal immutability of man when he said (Eccl. 3:14), "I know that, whatsoever God doeth, it shall be for ever: nothing can be put to it, nor any thing taken from it." In this truth lies man's God-given integrity and security.

If the one liar insistently suggests that another mortal, dear to us, has died and that a burden of grief has settled on us, what is Truth's answer? This, that right when this event claimed to have a place in our, his, or her, experience, right then the only fact was and is God's uninvadable universe of indestructible Life and its forever continuing identities. In this universe mortal mind and its perishable sense of mortal selfhood, with its birth and death, are unknown. The alone verity was and is the unbroken continuity of divine manifestation, in which every individual expression of Life, God, must ever remain inseparable from every other in the eternal symphony of indivisible Love.

If somewhere in its dream picture of material history evil says it has made a mortal, then tempted him with sin and enslaved him, how may the human being free himself from this enslavement? With his God-given spiritual sense he can discover and understand that the only man that is factual has never been materially conceived, tempted, or sin-enslaved. Because right when the one liar was arguing that this sequence of human events was taking place, right then God was the continuous, sinless Soul and Life of all individuality. Real selfhood was ever outside of lifeless, mindless mortal mind and its substratum, matter, and natively within the sinless, intelligent Mind, perfectly satisfied with his pure God-manifesting identity.

These demonstrable spiritual facts must be not

only persistently acclaimed but felt, loved, and lived. In the degree that this is done, the false, material sense of origin and its sequel, material history, will necessarily lessen. Man's unbroken continuity as God's everlasting witness—birthless, sinless, deathless—will then progressively come to light.

Frequently, some physical disorder argues that it began with some untoward experience in what evil says is one's past material history. Strain, fear, irritation, dark and morbid or critical thinking, are some of the lies from which evil would claim to fabricate forms of affliction. But what is talking and what is listening? Only the false material mind. Has its discordant medley of negatives supplanted for an instant the concordant, infinite, and eternal allness of God, good? No, God is constantly causing all of His children to express Him, the great I AM.

Right when the serpent talks to a state of material-mindedness, right then God is the only Mind. Actually, neither God nor man ever fears, feels, or knows a single afflictive suggestion of the evil one. The suppositional force of these suggestions spends itself in the vacuity of error's falsity; and this is true of the entire sum of suggestions that would constitute material history.

A case of insanity, of some years' standing, was healed when the spiritual fact was realized that the individual had never been born of, or embodied in, matter. Therefore, his mental faculties had never been impaired when he was thrown from a horse, with resulting injury to the material brain. Only the finger of evil drew this picture. It was a scene in a mortal's material history which the lying material mind said was this one's selfhood. Spirit, God, had no part in it. It therefore could not be true. The insanity had to give way before the understanding that man's Mind-faculties are as immune from evil suggestions as is the Mind that makes these faculties.

Evil claims to relate many physical and mental disorders to discordant human relationships in homes, society, business, all incident to the material history of men. But once again evil is building its case on totally false premises: that the material mind is the maker of man, that it erroneously impels, or projects, him into relationships that result in friction, oppression, injustice, animosity, and bring on physical or mental ills.

If one so troubled would find freedom from such ills, he should well digest this truth stated by Mrs. Eddy on page 262 of *Science and Health*: "The foundation of mortal discord is a false sense of man's origin. To begin rightly is to end rightly." The converse is equally true: to begin wrongly is to end wrongly. The Science of Life requires one to begin his reasoning rightly in the matter of relationship as in all other matters.

Problems arising from discordant relationships have their answer in the eternal facts of being. Right when evil claimed it made one its mortal puppet and subsequently related him unhappily to other mortals with resulting inharmony, what was the alone fact? Just this: that right then the one, true God was causing all identified manifestations of Himself and was intelligently relating them all to one another after the manner of Love's appointing.

To have order and unity in God's infinite, eternal kingdom, must not the Father of all forever harmoniously relate all ideas to each other? Does not Paul state simply the unchanging truth concerning relationship thus (Eph. 2:22): "Ye . . . are builded together for an habitation of God"?

Are not all the children of God eternally and harmoniously related to Him, and by Him wisely and peacefully related to one another, each knowing and rejoicing in his Love-ordered status?

Any individual who is willing consistently to use his God-given spiritual sense to discover the already existing harmony that characterizes God's universal family can begin to realize his freedom from the lie of evil that he is, or that anyone is or ever has been, an unhappily related mortal, since no such selfhood is his or his brother's.

Not his brother, but his own ignorant misconception of God and man, of cause and effect, he will discover, is the basic source of his trouble. The Christ, the true idea of God and man, will be to him his Saviour as it illumines his consciousness with the understanding of God's fatherhood, expressed in man's brotherhood. "In the habitation of dragons, where each lay, shall be grass with reeds and rushes" (Isa. 35:7).

Christian Science is here to help men find and demonstrate the pure monotheism taught by Christ Jesus: one infinite good and eternal God containing man, individually and collectively, in His uninvadable kingdom. As we cling steadfastly to this verity, we find that no matter what the aggressive suggestions of evil may be saying about the projection of evil into our experience, they lie, for they can do nothing else.

Right when evil claims to have a toe hold in God's infinity, right then God is infinite and All, and man's individuality is, as eternally, of and in Him. Nought but the one Spirit, Mind, can be cause to man at any moment in eternity. God never abandons His own son to the deceptions and villainies of material history. Nought can ever be the life and history of man save what is of deific Mind's conceiving.

—*Paul Stark Seeley*

SCRIPTURAL PROPHECY AND ITS FULFILLMENT

*C*hristian Science is lifting Christendom's concept of Scriptural prophecy from the level of what is more or less mystical to the position of the foretelling of the natural operation of divine law. Our beloved Leader, Mary Baker Eddy, has given us this definition of *prophet* in the Christian Science textbook, *Science and Health with Key to the Scriptures* (p. 593): "A spiritual seer; disappearance of material sense before the conscious facts of spiritual Truth."

The teachings of Christian Science include the basic truths that God's creation is spiritual and perfect; that the correct concept of His creation can be perceived only by means of spiritual sense, for the five corporeal senses present a false, mortal view of all things. Christian Science declares that what the world calls matter is an illusion; that actually it is the substratum of material thinking, evolved and sustained by the very senses, alias mortal mind, which behold it.

A prophet, according to Mrs. Eddy's definition already quoted, is anyone who forsakes the material sense of any situation or thing and beholds in place of it the spiritual fact as it exists in absolute scientific reality. This exalted view of Truth is prophecy in its highest scientific sense. It dispels the illusion of matter much as the sun's warm rays disperse a damp and gloomy mist. Truth demonstrates the superiority of its own true nature, and material sense eventually disappears, leaving unveiled the ever-present, eternal, spiritual reality.

The prophets of the Scriptural records were men of profound spiritual vision. Reflecting in a goodly measure Mind's omniscience, they evidently not only had clear glimpses of creation as it eternally exists in absolute reality, but also saw with startling accuracy the future mode of unfoldment by which the human consciousness would yield to the revealed truth. They perceived the conflict which this truth would engender, the resistance it would meet, and its inevitable triumph.

We have Scriptural authority for concluding that although centuries may intervene between the vision of spiritual reality and its full acceptance by the so-called human consciousness, the spiritual forces of prophetic fulfillment continue to evidence the majestic self-assertion of Deity, which no suppositional power of evil can frustrate or turn back. Once the clear view of spiritual truth has been discerned, every false belief which seems to prevent it from being a present established fact begins to disappear. What God knows is divine reality and is destined to be perceived as such by all men.

Christ Jesus recognized that his coming was in fulfillment of Scriptural prophecy. He quoted the prophets, read the prophetic Scriptures to his followers, and insisted upon a recognition of his own place in the fulfillment of prophecy. On numerous occasions he declared that the Scriptures must be fulfilled. So important did he deem the fulfillment of Scriptural prophecy that we find him expounding his place in it even after his resurrection. His authority must be seen as of God, else his mission is misunderstood, his God-inspired commands are disregarded, his divinely derived teachings ignored and neglected by mankind. "Search the scriptures," said Christ Jesus (John 5:39), "for in them ye think ye have eternal life: and they are they which testify of me."

Prophecy and its fulfillment are of profound interest to this age, inasmuch as it has witnessed unquestionable fulfillment of Scriptural prophecy in the appearing of the Comforter as revealed to Mary Baker Eddy and given to the world in her writings. The question is often asked, Why did Mrs. Eddy discover Christian Science and write the Christian Science textbook? Why did not some other individual—a man, perhaps—bring this final revelation of spiritual truth to mankind? The answer lies in the fact that God appoints His own messengers through law; that is, God inevitably declares His Word through the consciousness most ready to accept and proclaim it.

Students of Christian Science today are following the command of the Master to search the Scriptures. Therein they find prophecies of the coming of Christian Science, the final dispensation of divine law that demonstrates the womanhood of the divine nature, which from earliest prophecy was destined to bruise the head of the serpent, lust (Gen. 3:15). It was inevitable that a woman should be its revelator, for woman, suffering most from the false belief of human parenthood, is first to rise into the understanding of God's motherhood and of man's incorporeal, divine sonship, which Science reveals.

In many Scriptural passages the coming of Christian Science was hinted; but the Galilean Prophet, the master Christian, prophesied its appearing with vivid clarity. He described it as "the Comforter, which is the Holy Ghost, whom the Father will send in my name," and said, "He shall teach you all things, and bring all things to your remembrance, whatsoever I have said unto you" (John 14:26). From these words it is evident that an interpreter of the teachings of Christ Jesus was destined to appear. Later, in his glorious revelation to John, there is prophesied the coming of "a woman clothed with the sun, and the moon under her feet, and upon her head a crown of twelve stars" (Rev. 12:1). The woman is also pictured as being in travail, and as bringing forth "a man child, who was to rule all nations with a rod of iron" (verse 5). Christian Science explains this man child as the immaculate idea of divine Mind, the image of the Father-Mother, God, which Science unveils.

Mrs. Eddy has explained the threefold symbolism of the woman in the Apocalypse much as she has pointed out the twofold symbolism of the Lamb of Scriptural prophecy as standing for the eternal Christ and also for the human Jesus crucified (*Science and Health*, p. 334). In the Christian Science textbook we read (p. 561), "The woman in the Apocalypse symbolizes generic man, the spiritual idea of God;" and on page 562 the woman is referred to as "typifying the spiritual idea of God's motherhood." Of the third symbolism we read (*ibid.*), "Also the spiritual idea is typified by a woman in travail, waiting to be delivered of her sweet promise, but remembering no more her sorrow for joy that the birth goes on; for great is the idea, and the travail portentous."

Christian Scientists joyfully acclaim that these prophecies have been fulfilled in the life and works of Mrs. Eddy. She reveals in her works generic man, the incorporeal, complete manifestation or idea of divine Life. She unveils the motherhood of God, bringing the healing, mother touch of Love into the experience of countless multitudes. And our Leader's experience typified the woman in travail, the human messenger of Truth to this age, suffering, but suffering with joy in her presentation of the final revelation of real being to Soul-hungry humanity.

In order to gain a correct estimate of Mrs. Eddy's position in the fulfillment of Scriptural prophecies, it is necessary to understand how the momentum of prophetic fulfillment gathered force throughout the centuries following their utterance. When God's law of prophetic fulfillment attained in human consciousness the fullness of recognition sufficient for His spiritual requirement, the discovery and founding of Christian Science were made possible.

Mrs. Eddy's purity of nature and her ability to triumph over adverse circumstances were far more than mere personal virtues; they constituted, rather, the final yielding to divine law that fitted into the pattern of prophecy's fulfillment. They were incidental to the discovery of divine Science rather than causative. Her discovery had its roots in the ages, roots which went deeper than the personal sufferings of the Discoverer, her family inheritance of moral integrity, her Puritan ancestry, or her racial proclivities.

Our Leader says (*The First Church of Christ, Scientist, and Miscellany*, p. 178), "This Science is the essence of religion, distilled in the laboratory of infinite Love and prepared for all peoples." Because Christian Science was the exact culminating point of the fine distillation of Love's self-revealing forces, no other individual was prepared to be the Discoverer of Christian Science and the author of its spiritually revealed textbook. No other, therefore, can ever take Mrs. Eddy's place as the Leader of the Christian Science movement or destroy the continuing spirit of that leadership as expressed in her *Manual of The Mother Church*.

Mrs. Eddy was the God-appointed messenger of Truth to this age. Future generations await humanity's full appreciation of this fact. She cannot be separated from her revelation. Inability to demonstrate Christian Science has often been traced to an insufficient appreciation of the true position of its revelator, or to a failure to handle a secret antagonism to her personality which seems to present itself in devious ways to the unwary.

Christian Science is the "Spirit of truth" (John 14:17), the law which links the ages in the demonstration of the ever-present Christ. Today, through Mrs. Eddy's precious ministrations, Truth stands fully revealed for all men to practice. Every Christian Scientist is a prophet in the degree that his vision of spiritual reality is sufficiently clear to dispel the illusion of error and reveal the presence of eternal Truth. Every Christian Science demonstration is, in that degree, prophecy fulfilled.

The definition of *Elias* given in our textbook

is as follows (*Science and Health*, p. 585): "Prophecy; spiritual evidence opposed to material sense; Christian Science, with which can be discerned the spiritual fact of whatever the material senses behold; the basis of immortality. 'Elias truly shall first come and restore all things.' (Matthew xvii. 11)." Christian Science is restoring all things, is replacing false beliefs with spiritual facts. Scriptural prophecy is still in process of fulfillment in the lives of those who help "the woman" (Rev. 12:16), those who understand and demonstrate the divine ideas which Mrs. Eddy revealed. It will be completely fulfilled only when the Science of being is fully demonstrated. Then man will be seen as eternally loving God supremely and his neighbor as himself. Wars will cease, matter will disappear, and God's children will all be known in their primeval, sinless perfection, the image and likeness of their heavenly Father-Mother, God.

—Helen Wood Bauman

"THE SMELL OF FIRE"

Perhaps there is no story more dear to the heart of the Christian Scientist than that of the deliverance of the three young Hebrew captives from Nebuchadnezzar's fiery furnace (see Daniel 3). It is, indeed, so familiar to all of us, even to those who have hitherto been only casual readers of the Bible, that it needs no repetition here. There is one point, however, in connection with it which, though often dwelt upon, has particularly interested at least one student of Christian Science of late, and it is this: that after Shadrach, Meshach, and Abed-nego were finally released, not only were their clothes unhurt and the hair of their heads unsinged, but not even "the smell of fire had passed on them."

"The smell of fire,"—that is where one endeavoring to understand the Scriptures in their true spiritual meaning and import may well give pause; for what, metaphysically speaking, is the smell of the fire? Is it not the remembrance of it, the sting of it, the resentment over it? "The smell of fire" is the acknowledgment that an evil happened. It means that evil has a history. It means that although the fire is out now, it once existed, and we were in it. So insistently does this last argument seem to cling to consciousness that some of us go through the fire and every one smells smoke on us for years afterwards. When such is the case, can it be said that we, like those three of long ago, have come through the experience untouched?

Let us refuse to allow error to attach itself to us in any way, shape, or manner. Its claim that it once had activity, presence, power, cause, intelligence, or law is a false and spurious claim, and should be seen and handled only as its last, desperate effort, since all else has failed, to get itself perpetuated as a belief of memory. Let us refuse to give it life, even to that extent. Let us refuse to admit that evil ever had either a beginning or an ending. Let us refuse to admit that it ever was at all, even for one unholy moment. This, of course, by no means implies that we should not give grateful thanks for our deliverance from the belief in it, at the right time and in the right place, with the pure desire to help some one else who may be going through a similar experience. It only means that it does not facilitate the elimination of "the smell of fire" from our garments if we drag the remembrance of it around with us wherever we go, brooding over it unnecessarily in private, talking of it unnecessarily in public, and seeming to take a melancholy delight in recounting its unpleasant details. Will it daily grow beautifully less by any such procedure?

In the warfare which is wholly spiritual there should be no wounded veterans pointing to their scars with pardonable pride, simply because, if the fighting has been rightly done, there will be no scars to exhibit. "Trials are proofs of God's care," as we are told in *Science and Health with Key to the Scriptures* by Mary Baker Eddy (p. 66), and surely it is not in accord with the nature of Love that, when a proof of this tender care is given, the incident should be seared upon us with a permanent stamp of past suffering. God's ways are painless, easy, gentle, natural. It is only our rebellion over learning our much needed lessons which causes any suffering. Little children at school do not necessarily suffer and get scarred for life just because they pass from the Primer Class into the First Reader. Let us refuse to be scarred-up Christian Scientists. We do not have to be. Let us just be Christian Scientists who have learned our lessons and gone up higher.

Perhaps, however, that which most commonly keeps alive "the smell of fire" is self-pity. We feel so sorry for ourselves, forgetting that thereby we encourage others to feel sorry for us, since one seldom fails to receive that for which he makes a market. Jesus said, "The prince of this world cometh, and hath nothing in me" (John 14:30). When the "prince of this world" presents himself at the door of any human consciousness, he cannot effect an entrance unless there is something in that consciousness which responds. He may come over and over, but if he meets with no response he will soon get tired of coming. There is a limit to the length of time when even the most persistent falsity will continue to knock at a door resolutely closed and barred against it. Let us tire error out, instead of letting it tire us out.

As for the pity of others for us, there are few things more dully stupefying than sympathetic mesmerism. Human sympathy tends to strangle its victim in the python coil of what it impudently calls "love." Under its influence even that high and holy thing called "mother love" has sometimes been perverted into that which might better be termed "smother love." Yet one often unconsciously comes down under it because it assumes that phase of evil hardest to detect, namely, evil coming in the name of good, something which puts Christian Scientists off their guard more quickly than anything else in the world. Evil coming in the name of evil fights in the open. We see it in all its hideous proportions, recognize it for what it is, and govern ourselves accordingly; but evil coming in the name of good puts on the habiliments of heaven, presents itself to the guard in this stolen uniform, gives the countersign "love," and slips into the camp undetected.

One of the best antidotes for self-pity, should one ever find himself inclined to indulge in it, has been given by our revered Leader in *Miscellaneous Writings* (p. 18): "Thou shalt recognize thyself as God's spiritual child only, and the true man and true woman, the all-harmonious 'male and female' as of spiritual origin, God's reflection,—thus as children of one common Parent,—wherein and whereby Father, Mother, and child are the divine Principle and divine idea, even the divine 'Us'—one in good, and good in One." This inspired statement certainly strips off error's disguise in an instant, and leaves it cowering and ashamed before Truth; for if we once recognize ourselves in this our true identity and being, what is there left to pity or to be pitied? Is "God's spiritual child" ever an object of commiseration? Are we mortals or immortals? Of course we can think of ourselves as mortals if we choose. Nobody is going to stop us; indeed mortal mind would gladly encourage us in the delusion. Our false estimate of ourselves, however, and the world's false estimate of us can never for one instant change the forever fact that "now are we the sons of God" (I John 3:2).

There is something else, however, besides self-pity which helps to keep alive "the smell of fire," and that is self-condemnation. Either one alone is bad enough; but when they go hand in hand, as they so often do, one might as well step back into his fiery furnace and stay there a while longer; for his demonstration is not made. Does that sound discouraging? Perhaps, just at first; but when one is "speaking the truth in love," as the apostle so beautifully puts it, no one can feel really the worse for having heard it (Eph. 4:15). Let us be awake to this fallacy of self-condemnation. Like its boon companion, it presupposes that evil has a history, and that we were identified with it. It tricks us first into admitting that there was a fiery furnace heated "seven times more than it was wont to be heated," for our especial benefit. This much conceded, it argues to us that we were once in it, and that we did get out of it finally, but not so quickly nor so gracefully nor so spectacularly as it now makes us believe we should have done, or as anybody else would have done under the same circumstances.

Let us refuse to accept any argument that perpetuates a belief in a material past. To hold a post-mortem over error is tacitly to admit that it once had life. Why not forget "those things which are behind," as the apostle says, and press forward (Phil. 3:13)? Let us shut the door on condemnation, both from within and from without. What other people say about our experience matters little, so long as God understands. Unless those who may now be criticizing stood right beside us in the furnace all through it, they are in no position to judge how hot the fire was.

What a wonderful thing it would be if every one who had ever passed through a trying ordeal would come out of it "every whit whole," with head erect and with shining eyes, with a greater love for God and man, a deeper gratitude, a stronger faith; and with a broader charity for the mistakes and struggles of the weak and weary ones of earth! What a goodly company they would make, these purified ones, as they go their silent way among us, peaceful, exalted, chastened, humble, their faces still radiant with the joy of demonstration!

Since our Leader tells us that "those only who are tried in the furnace reflect the image of their Father" (*Miscellaneous Writings*, p. 278), should we ever look back upon any such experience with anything but gratitude? "Beloved," wrote the apostle Peter, from the depths of his own personal experience, "think it not strange concerning the fiery trial which is to try you, as though some strange thing happened unto you: but rejoice, inasmuch as ye are partakers of Christ's sufferings; that, when his glory shall be revealed, ye may be glad also with exceeding joy . . . for the spirit of glory and of God resteth upon you" (I Pet. 4:12–14).

"The spirit of glory and of God"! To gain that, is it not worth a few pangs, or many pangs, if need be? Let us never forget that it was right there, in the midst of the fire, that those captives of long ago saw the vision of the Christ. Their human extremity was so great that they rose to a mental height born of the necessity of the moment, and beheld man as he really is, spiritual and not material, and beheld this saving fact so plainly that even the dull eyes of the watching Nebuchadnezzar caught the vision. "Did not we cast three men bound into the midst of the fire?" he cried in amazement; "Lo, I see four men loose, walking in the midst of the fire, and they have no hurt; and the form of the fourth is like the Son of God."

That heavenly glimpse of divine reality, that

clear realization of man as he really is, "the Son of God," is not so often gained in our hours of ease as in those testing times when the utmost efforts of animal magnetism seem put forth to destroy the Christ-idea for which we stand. So let us rejoice, even if it were through great tribulation that we gained the vision; for "the form of the fourth" once seen, can never be forgotten, nor can we ever go back to where we were before the wonder and the glory of it came. So the fire goes out, the princes, governors, captains, and counselors depart in baffled fury, Nebuchadnezzar openly proclaims that "there is no other God that can deliver after this sort," and those "upon whose bodies the fire had no power" quietly go about their business.

If the demonstration has been a perfect one, clean-cut, permanent, convincing, this is what he who has just been released will naturally say if questioned about his experience, and if he can say it in very truth and mean it, he may be absolutely sure that even "the smell of fire" is gone: "Was it hard? I don't know. The vision was so beautiful I have forgotten all the rest."

—Louise Knight Wheatley

Supply as Spiritual Reflection

~

*M*an has supply because he reflects God. The first chapter of Genesis states that God made man in His own image and after His likeness. Christian Science is the glorious discovery of the great truth, namely, that man is the full and perfect expression of God. Such being the fact, man has nothing underived from God, nor can he, as God's reflection, be incomplete or lack in any degree that which God includes. Therefore, man manifests supply, and, furthermore, supply is wholly spiritual.

The human mind challenges this statement. So imbued is it with the belief that supply is material, and that it comes to the individual through material channels and toilsome effort rather than from within, through spiritual discernment and divine reflection, that it seems difficult for the human consciousness to accept the statement that in reflecting Life, man reflects all that constitutes Life. Like the man in Jesus' parable who pulled down his barns and built greater, and said to his soul, "Thou hast much goods laid up for many years" (Luke 12:19), mortals seek security in material possessions, only to find them fleeting, insecure, and illusory. Then they believe themselves to be in lack. Every manifestation of lack is but an illusion of fear, of ignorance, or of sin.

Spiritual supply flows directly from God to man; or, more accurately stated, it coexists with God and man. It requires no human avenue or channel in order to be made manifest. Man in God's image can no more be separated from supply than he can be separated from God, for all that man has, all that man is, is the reflection of God.

When to human sense supply appears to be cut off or obstructed, either temporarily or permanently; when there appears to be no human source or avenue whatever through which supply can come, it will be made manifest when God is spiritually and scientifically understood, as witness Jesus' demonstration of the loaves and fishes. Man is not a channel for God, but a manifestation of God. He is more than the recipient of good; he is the expression of good. Man is not something through which or to which God flows; he is the very expression or evidence of God.

The love of money rests on the tyranny, the despotism, of materialism. It is that which says, Without me—matter—you can do nothing, not even live! Rightly considered, money is a medium of exchange, a symbol of gratitude, something given in return for value received. Instead of asking oneself, "How much money have I?" one would do well to consider, How much gratitude have I?

In its finite concept of supply, the human mind forever measures and limits that which it deems good and indispensable. Christian Science demands of its students a radical change in thinking. The sun does not say, If only I had not shone quite so much yesterday, I should have more light with which to shine today. The fact that it shone yesterday is the proof that it can shine today. Yet mortals are prone to say, "If I had not spent so much yesterday," or even, "If I had not given so much yesterday, I should have more today." Such reasoning is based on matter and does not recognize Mind as the inexhaustible source of supply, and man as infinite reflection. Neither the good we did yesterday nor the seeming mistakes and failures of yesterday limit or darken today, except in so far as ignorant, false belief permits. It never occurs to us that the one who has passed beyond this plane of existence is cut off from supply, although every human avenue through which it came to him here is left behind. Neither can we be cut off from divine supply here and now.

In reality, supply has never been too generously shared, nor has it ever been squandered or unwisely invested. Being spiritual it is indivisible, and it coexists in its completeness with God and man. There have never been any mistakes or misjudgments in God's universe. Since no mistake ever really occurred in the past, it can bring no real consequence in the present. Supply is man's today by reason of his relationship to God. He has eternal supply because he reflects God. No evidence before the material senses can alter this fact. In Truth, there are no lost opportunities, no past mistakes. Man is the present reflection of God.

If we would increase our human manifestation of supply, we must cultivate the habit of magnifying good. The human mind is prone to magnify evil; it holds to, recounts, and magnifies every disturbing incident. Alert students of Christian Science are seeing good multiply in their experience through the habitual attitude of minimizing evil and magnifying good. Which are we seeing—Love's abundance or error's want?

Strictly speaking, no one is ever without income. Something is coming into our thought every moment, either suggestions of loss, lack, impoverishment, fear, dismay, or spiritual ideas which acknowledge God and man's relationship to Him. We need to watch our thoughts carefully, for according to them the outward manifestation will be poverty or abundance.

Supply is not outlined or limited by the figures in a bankbook or the amount of a salary. Supply is as infinite and indivisible as God Himself. We must expand our thinking. Mortal limitations are self-imposed. Let us refuse to be mesmerized. In all God's universe there is no such thing as lack. No one can limit abundance to himself. Each can demonstrate it, and by so doing he is proving it to be a demonstrable fact for every child of God. We should not speak of "my" supply, or "your" supply, any more than we speak of "my" sunshine, or "your" sunshine. It is just sunshine, abundant sunshine, and each may enjoy just as much of it as he chooses, if he takes the trouble to go out into it, without limiting or depriving anyone else.

Human reasoning looks anxiously ahead and says, At such and such a time my income, or part of it, may stop. God knows nothing about calendars, nothing about changes. Supply is continuous. The haunting fear of material supply and material lack will vanish before the scientific demonstration of man's relationship to God. In this relationship there is no stagnation, no obstruction, no unrequited, labored effort. Man reflects. He does not toil. Says the Apostle John, "Beloved, now are we the sons of God" (I John 3:2). And Paul says, "We are the children of God: and if children, then heirs; heirs of God, and joint-heirs with Christ" (Rom. 8:16–17).

Christian Science teaches that these truths relative to man's abundant present supply should be demonstrated as one spends or incurs obligations, for they are spiritual facts which it is our birthright to demonstrate. Such demonstration rests on honesty, purity, unselfish desire. Let no one think he can demonstrate supply in Christian Science for selfish gain or the gratification of sense. Scientific thinking is thinking that is in line with Principle. This results in a proper sense of values. It takes away both the love of material possession and the fear of material lack. "Our sufficiency is of God" (II Cor. 3:5). Mortal mind's lying, mesmeric argument is always insufficiency. The one with the largest bank account may be the one with the greatest sense of insufficiency. In reality the only demands made upon man are spiritual demands. Mind makes them and fulfills them. Man reflects the infinitude of Mind—hence his sufficiency.

Mortal mind always begins from the wrong end of a problem in seeking its solution. Anxious retrenchment and curtailment, while sometimes humanly necessary, never demonstrate abundance. The very fact of entertaining such a finite mental concept limits one's sense of supply, and therefore cannot demonstrate sufficiency. The position achieved through scientific demonstration can be held. There is no reversal. There is no retrograde step. Error's argument is retrogression. Truth's command is, "Go forward!" This applies to finances, home, church, health—activity and usefulness in all their forms. Good is not attained negatively. Truth is affirmative. Principle is positive. We never advance through negative thinking. Christian Science demands that we keep our thinking positive.

In *Science and Health with Key to the Scriptures* Mary Baker Eddy writes (p. 258), "Man reflects infinity, and this reflection is the true idea of God." And she continues, "God expresses in man the infinite idea forever developing itself, broadening and rising higher and higher from a boundless basis." As each individual learns through Christian Science to appropriate this truth, and grows in the spiritual understanding of God to the point where he can demonstrate it, this statement will be found to epitomize the permanent, positive solution of the question of supply.

—L. Ivimy Gwalter

TARGET OUT OF RANGE

A practitioner of Christian Science was called to the home of one in distress. The sufferer was a Reader in a branch Church of Christ, Scientist. She was convinced that because of this she was a target for mortal mind's hatred of Truth. The practitioner seemed unable to persuade the patient otherwise. Finally the practitioner said: "Well, if you will be a target, be one. But, for goodness' sake, be a target out of range."

A target out of range! What vistas this opens. To be out of range is to be out of reach, beyond the limited shafts of the aggressor. The bird has but to spread its wings and mount to azure heights to be beyond the range of the sharpshooter.

Can we be as fetterless and free as the bird? Of course we can. The beloved Discoverer and Founder of Christian Science, Mary Baker Eddy, pointing to man's inherent freedom, writes in *Science and Health with Key to the Scriptures* (p. 223), "Sooner or later we shall learn that the fetters of man's finite capacity are forged by the illusion that he lives in body instead of in Soul, in matter instead of in Spirit." Fetters forged by illusion are illusions, not realities.

Christ Jesus found his safety in claiming the spirituality of his being. It is recorded in the Gospel of Luke that on one occasion as he taught in the synagogue his hearers were filled with wrath. They rose up and cast him out and led him to the brow of a hill, intending to throw him down headlong. But he passed through the midst of them and went his way, undisturbed in his healing ministry. They did not even see him. He prophesied that those who believed on him would do the works that he did, and even greater works, "because I go unto my Father" (John 14:12). Mrs. Eddy says (*Miscellaneous Writings*, pp. 195–196), "The 'I' will go to the Father when meekness, purity, and love, informed by divine Science, the Comforter, lead to the one God: then the ego is found not in matter but in Mind, for there is but one God, one Mind; and man will then claim no mind apart from God."

So long as we identify ourselves as finite persons appointed by other persons to hold certain offices or perform certain tasks in our movement, just so long do we lay ourselves open to being targets,

suppositious victims of hatred, envy, deception, and hypnotic control. Opposition and criticism, discouragement and inefficiency, often follow in the train of these errors. But mortal mind never reaches beyond itself. It sees itself, its own mistaken concept of itself, condemns itself, destroys itself. Neither God nor the real man is ever within range of materialism.

Aggressive mental suggestion may whisper: "You are a mortal. I, evil, can make you afraid, make you sick, wear you out, exhaust you. I can besmirch your character, belie your integrity, and cause others to believe and circulate these lies. In spite of your best efforts, I can make you feel incompetent, mistrusted, unloved, unhappy." Or the aggressive suggestion may raise its voice in self-justification and under the guise of our own thought argue: "I am important. I demand to be recognized. I want my own way and intend to do my own will." But neither self-depreciation nor self-glorification is real, and the alert Christian Scientist does not lend himself as the tool of either one. He does not let error use him to bring dissension, division, or disloyalty into our movement. He does not allow himself to be handled by lack of wisdom, self-seeking pride, or a false sense of martyrdom. His surety is in God, and his joy no man takes from him.

When we stop to think about it, where are we more safe, more loved, more cherished, than in the service of our Maker? Where may we more sensibly feel the self-renewal of Life, the strength of Truth, the nourishment of Love? Let "meekness, purity, and love, informed by divine Science" cleanse us of the egotistical belief of being a mortal and lift thought above matter to Spirit. Then in true humility shall we acknowledge Mind as the Ego, the I of our being, and comprehend more deeply the Master's sayings: "He that cometh from above is above all" (John 3:31); "The Father himself, which hath sent me, hath borne witness of me" (John 5:37); "I and my Father are one" (John 10:30).

In the uncontaminated realm of Spirit and from the standpoint of God's allness, man's lifework unfolds as the subjective experience of divine Mind. Soul reveals its own grandeur and glory, Love its own peace and poise. In Science, man reflects God and is unconstrained, unhindered, unbounded. He is not localized and finitized; hence he cannot influence erroneously or be so influenced. Life expresses its own full, free course of resplendent Life, and man is its expression. Hence man rejoices in the limitless capacity of his God-derived being, exempt from accident, age, decay.

God never made a law of penalty nor made man capable of experiencing penalty. God's law is the law of freedom, the law of justice, the law of Love. Says Mrs. Eddy in *Science and Health* (pp. 513–514), "So-called mortal mind—being non-existent and consequently not within the range of immortal existence—could not by simulating deific power invert the divine creation, and afterwards recreate persons or things upon its own plane, since nothing exists beyond the range of all-inclusive infinity, in which and of which God is the sole creator." And she adds, "Mind, joyous in strength, dwells in the realm of Mind."

In the realization of this fact we are indeed a target out of range—no target—for nothing exists but the forever all-inclusiveness of everlasting Love, and man abides in the consciousness of Love, as Mind's eternal expression of its own self-completeness and unbroken harmony.

Darkness never pierces light, but light extinguishes darkness. To light all is, without interruption, forever light. In "meekness, purity, and love, informed by divine Science," let us see that the "I" does go to the Father—is indeed forever one with the Father—and so let us know ourselves as the unassailable radiance of His presence.

—*L. Ivimy Gwalter*

"Teach me to love."

There was a time when in my daily prayer
I asked for all the things I deemed most fair,
And necessary to my life,—success,
Riches, of course, and ease, and happiness;
A host of friends, a home without alloy;
A primrose path of luxury and joy,
Social distinction, and enough of fame
To leave behind a well-remembered name.

Ambition ruled my life. I longed to do
Great things, that all my little world might view
And whisper, "Wonderful!"
                            Ah, patient God,
How blind we are, until Thy shepherd's rod
Of tender chastening gently leads us on
To better things! To-day I have but one
Petition, Lord—Teach me to love. Indeed,
It is my greatest and my only need—
Teach me to love, not those who first love me,
But all the world, with that rare purity
Of broad, outreaching thought which bears no trace
Of earthly taint, but holds in its embrace
Humanity, and only seems to see
The good in all, reflected, Lord, from Thee.

And teach me, Father, how to love the most
Those who most stand in need of love—that host
Of people who are sick and poor and bad,
Whose tired faces show their lives are sad,
Who toil along the road with footsteps slow,
And hearts more heavy than the world can know—
People whom others pass discreetly by,
Or fail to hear the pleading of that cry
For help, amid the tumult of the crowd;
Whose very anguish makes them cold and proud,
Resentful, stubborn, bitter in their grief—
I want to bring them comfort and relief,
To put my hand in theirs, and at their side
Walk softly on, a faithful, fearless guide.
O Saviour, thou the Christ, Truth, ever near,
Help me to feel these sad ones doubly dear
Because they need so much! Help me to seek
And find that which they thought was lost; to speak
Such words of cheer that as we pass along
The wilderness shall blossom into song.

Ah, Love divine, how empty was that prayer
Of other days! That which was once so fair,—
Those flimsy baubles which the world calls joys
Are nothing to me now but broken toys,
Outlived, outgrown. I thank Thee that I know
Those much-desired dreams of long ago,
Like butterflies, have had their summer's day
Of brief enchantment, and have gone. I pray
For better things.
                        Thou knowest, God above,
My one desire now—Teach me to love.

—*Louise Knight Wheatley*

THERE IS HOPE!

*T*hose who have not yet found Christian Science and its comforting assurance in these days of mounting human turmoil and misgiving might understandably echo the anguished and poignant cry recorded in Jeremiah (8:20, 22): "The harvest is past, the summer is ended, and we are not saved… Is there no balm in Gilead; is there no physician there?"

To the distressed queries of mankind today, Christian Scientists are responding with a loving, affirmative, "Yes, there is balm; there is healing; there is hope!" Of all people in this critical hour of human history Christian Scientists gratefully stand "ready always," in the words of Peter, "to give an answer to every man that asketh you a reason of the hope that is in you" (I Pet. 3:15). Christian Scientists could not do otherwise, for they have found a religion of assurance based on enduring and tangible proof of the blessings awaiting everyone who humbly and sincerely seeks day by day to embrace and truly live its teachings.

The priceless gift of spiritual understanding in the very midst of difficulties pressing for solution enabled Job to exclaim (Job 19:25), "I know that my redeemer liveth," and thence to achieve his own freedom, dominion, and peace. With this assurance of a knowable, intimate Redeemer of humanity, Christian Science often bestows its first gentle comfort upon the individual approaching this religion and its teachings for the first time. Multitudes of men and women, including the writer, have forsaken their trust in cynicism and negative "realism" and have taken their first firm hold upon Christian Science when they discovered that it is not mere optimism, not a humanly mental system or scheme of wishing oneself into well-being, or a veneering over of the troubles of the world with trite sentiments or emotional platitudes.

The hope of Christian Science is actual and tangible and holds out no ethereal panacea which, once reached for, only vanishes from the grasp of the yearning seeker for deliverance. The beneficent Discoverer and Founder of Christian Science, Mary Baker Eddy, who proved her holy mission by requiring it to be manifested in specific healing and fruitage, makes this unmistakably clear in *Science and Health with Key to the Scriptures* where she says (p. 367), "The tender word and Christian encouragement of an invalid, pitiful patience with his fears and the removal of them, are better than hecatombs of gushing theories, stereotyped borrowed speeches, and the doling of arguments, which are but so many parodies on legitimate Christian Science, aflame with divine Love."

No, the practice of Christian Science has no parallel in the philosophy of the well-meaning, fictional Pollyanna, urging everyone just to be "glad" without explaining how this may be achieved and maintained in the face of human enigma and frustration. Nor is the practice of Christian Science based on mental suggestion, incantation, or self-hypnotism as a means to health and peace. To the distraught and world-weary, Christian Science does not proffer the husks of glibness, shallow slogans, or bland homilies that neither nourish nor reassure. Nor does the Christian Scientist draw his hope, expectancy, and conviction merely from turning his back on evil. He does not emulate the two hunters depicted in a popular magazine cartoon. Lost in a tangled jungle without weapons and confronted by a mammoth, savage beast, one hunter tremblingly calls out to the other, "Let us just close our eyes and wait, and perhaps it will go away." Contrariwise, the "reason of the hope that is in" the Christian Scientist is based on spiritual understanding, which, in the words of James (5:16), is "the effectual fervent prayer of a righteous man [that] availeth much."

On this prayerful basis of thought and action the hope implicit in Christian Science does not falter or fail in the face of any test whatever of its depth and anchorage. "What," a student of Christian Science was once asked by a friend steeped in medical education and fear of its propaganda, "would you do if confronted by a serious disease?" Never for a moment accepting the query as a personal challenge, the student humbly replied: "Why, I would just be thankful that I could confidently and understandingly turn away from limited human resources to God's infinite spiritual resources, and I would be grateful that the same opportunity is always available for everyone to accept, particularly those who are told by their medical helpers that their condition is hopeless or incurable."

Here the uninformed investigator of Christian Science and its teachings may ask: "But how can I hope or feel expectant of God's deliverance when Deity is only a name or symbol to me, and when it is so obvious that futility, hopelessness, incurability, frustration, and dismal resignation to evil have chained me, and so many others like me?

What is there to indicate that the God I have never really known is even aware of my needs or those of humanity? What is there to hope for?"

Here Christian Science readily presents and explains the availability of enduring hope in terms that can truly satisfy because they are presently applicable and rational. Our Leader declares in *Science and Health* (p. 223), "Spiritual rationality and free thought accompany approaching Science, and cannot be put down." Now the seeker finds that the dawn of spiritual understanding in his consciousness awakens the hope of deliverance through the apprehension of divine reality in contradistinction to false material concepts of any name or nature. Therefore, hope in Christian Science becomes as rational as intelligent enlightenment, as realistic as positive conviction, as substantive as the fruitage which assuredly follows for those who turn unreservedly for deliverance to God—to God as Christian Science reveals His holy and perfect nature to those who love Him.

Even the medical practitioners of our day encourage the sick to be hopeful and of good cheer. The sick may ask under such circumstances, "Be hopeful of what, and of good cheer about what?" The answer is, "Nothing, so long as materialism and mortality draw bindingly tight the confines of one's expectancy of good." But hope is spiritual assurance and comes when consciousness turns with childlike trust to the infinite realm of Spirit, Mind, divine reality.

The consecrated Christian Scientist would be the first to acknowledge that there is little hope for men as long as that hope is based solely on material sense and the concept of an erratic existence, totally spanned by mortal birth, growth, maturity, death, and dissolution. But the Christian Scientist affirms at the same moment that there is indeed abundant hope, assured deliverance and redemption—in health, home, character, environment, supply, occupation, and all human relationships—for those who learn to know God as Spirit and to behold man and the universe as His spiritual, perfect reflection.

Why have not the purposeful and earnest hopes of sincere statesmen and humanitarians been realized in more heartening manifestations of progressive unification of nations, groups, communities, and organizations of human beings? Is it not because these hopes, however sincere, have nevertheless dealt with men and nations on the basis of the mortal and temporal dream of material existence and the pernicious belief of minds many, rather than in terms of one infinite Mind, God, and His infinite ideas, including the universe and man? One who understands this in Christian Science understands also that there is the fullest justification not only for hope but of absolute faith, leading to the spiritual comprehension of the true and indestructible destiny awaiting men and nations—the beauty of holiness, the perceptible goodness of God.

One's imperative first need, then, and indeed his inevitable standpoint of hope, is to begin to see the goodness of God as revealed to humanity by Mrs. Eddy in the seven synonymous terms which express His divine nature and allness: Mind, Soul, Spirit, Principle, Love, Truth, and Life. If we take the true nature of God to be one and only one—the I AM THAT I AM revealed to Moses—there is left nothing but the goodness and perfection of our Father-Mother God and His infinite resources on which to base our confident expectancy. How can this ever leave anyone hopeless or helpless, if one starts now to pray daily for the achievement of spiritual understanding, the consciousness of eternal reality?

Does the reader ever feel anything less than pride, satisfaction, and confidence in recommending to others an affluent and trusted friend of great moral character and accomplishment? How much more assuredly, then, and with what a deep sense of privilege, may we bring hope to the sick and needy and distressed by recommending to them God Himself and feel no personal responsibility or reservation whatever regarding the outcome of our action!

The earnest laborer in the vineyard of Christian Science is acutely aware of the opportunity and challenge implied in his prayerful daily effort to let the light which shines before men in his words and deeds be translated into hope for everyone whose life touches his in the round of day-to-day experience. The only measure of the effectiveness of this work, of course, is in the faithfulness of one's earnest purpose to live a life that blesses others with its spiritual prayerfulness rather than with words alone. More than once the writer has seen the need of remaining alert to fan the waning spark of hope in some friend perhaps unacquainted with Christian Science who, outwardly cheerful, was actually hiding a distressing fear or dread in the belief that there was no available remedy. The result of this alertness has been the opportunity to present Christian Science to more than a few who considered their situation hopeless and to witness the fruitage thereof.

In one of these instances, a fellow worker on a daily newspaper was accustomed frequently to mention Christian Science derisively to the writer, but never received an argumentative reply. One day this fellow worker, quite subdued and disheartened, suddenly announced that his doctor had just declared him to be afflicted with an incurable disease and stated that he would no longer be able to earn a livelihood in the newspaper profession. The writer quietly said, "Aren't you telling me this now so that I can show you that there is hope for you in Christian Science?"

"Yes," the friend haltingly replied, "I have nowhere else to turn."

Within a few hours he was following the directions given him: he visited a Reading Room, obtained the services of a Christian Science practitioner, and was healed. Today, twenty-six years later, he is a healthy and successful journalist.

How confidently may the working Christian Scientist sing the assuring song of hope given to men in the Psalm (42:11): "Why art thou cast down, O my soul? and why art thou disquieted within me? hope thou in God: for I shall yet praise him, who is the health of my countenance, and my God"!

—*John H. Hoagland*

THOUGHTS ON YOUR BUSINESS OR PROFESSION

*H*ere are some thoughts regarding business that have come to me over the years. The first is that everything belongs to God. The Psalmist declared, "The earth is the Lord's, and the fulness thereof" (Ps. 24:1). And Christ Jesus made this very clear: "Are not five sparrows sold for two farthings, and not one of them is forgotten before God? But even the very hairs of your head are all numbered. Fear not therefore" (Luke 12:6, 7).

So our real business or profession is in His hands. He owns and controls it. If you own the business you're in, see clearly that all that is real about it belongs to God, and you'll be immune to the burdens and responsibilities that seem inherent in the belief of ownership.

People sometimes think of the public practice of Christian Science as uniquely God's business. When I'm a practitioner, they think, I'll be working for God alone, and then I'll have absolute freedom of thought in handling my activity. But I remember the comment of a woman who had been in the business world for years. She remarked that she'd held several demanding positions, but that she'd always been unburdened in her thought. She knew she was working for God and felt free to serve Him. This was a lesson to me. I saw that freedom relative to an activity stems entirely from right thinking about it. We can be free in thought irrespective of our business or profession.

How wonderful that you're not *in* a certain business or profession! No business or position can think of you. You can think of it. So you're not in a certain business, but you include it in your thinking. And, looking deeper, you're bigger than any position or business, for you're a representative of infinite Mind. Your true business, or activity, is to be man, to express the qualities of that perfect Mind. Your human position is just the vehicle through which you bring this out humanly.

Most of us are accustomed to looking to our business or our position for supply. This is working backward. Your business doesn't really supply you. You supply it with ideas and ability. We turn to God for the ideas we bring to our work. There's no limit to the intelligence, ability, and inspiration the divine Mind is furnishing us with to conduct and prosper our activity.

In most occupations and activities we work with others, and sometimes we're faced with relationship problems. These would burden us, create confusion, and suggest false responsibility. Then what do we do about them? We begin our reasoning with God, one Mind, who creates all and holds all of His ideas in right relationship to each other. Ideas of the one Mind never conflict. So we see God's ideas as coordinate, as working together harmoniously under the government of the one Mind, which is Principle.

This true view of man, based on God, enables us to unsee temperamental errors exhibited by others. We make real progress in seeing and demonstrating that we and they alike are God's ideas, undisturbed in the consciousness of our oneness with omnipotent Principle. We find ourselves becoming superior to the tension, pressure, and drive of modern business.

Whatever our activity, we need to meet the aggressive suggestions of animal magnetism, of a supposed influence apart from God, that would claim to resist our progress. It's not people that hamper us, but the beliefs apparently using people, such as envy and domination. What matters is whether we let these beliefs use *us*. They have no power. They can't make us think our progress is subordinate to the business we're in or the officers over us. The truth is that the God-given progress of each one is independent of other people and of material conditions.

The one Mind understands but does not limit us. One might say that we limit ourselves, but that would be in belief only, since we express the one Mind. All we're faced with is opportunity—the opportunity of unseeing the errors that are claiming acceptance in our organization, and of perceiving the truths that are really there.

Then there's the problem of newness. Are our progressive concepts and plans meeting opposition just because they are "new"? Then let's recognize what they represent—Mind's creation, already established in Mind. In this sense we can go by the words of the wise man, "There is no new thing under the sun" (Eccl. 1:9).

Businessmen have erred in thinking of their concepts or propositions as new, unknown, unheard-of. Basically, the good they seek to further is already established, and knowing this, presenting one's plan accordingly, counteracts the resistance of mortal mind. In such a case one might well stress utility rather than newness. Nor does the wise businessman feel the human idea is peculiarly his own. He envisions it as emanating from divine wisdom, hence as usable by anyone. It has its work to do and will be justly judged.

Christian Science, applied, enables one to foresee and forestall the resistance of mortal mind to change and progress. This doesn't imply that a businessman shouldn't try different things; but consonant with the truth that there's nothing really new, he can work so as to eliminate the supposed hazards of newness—opposition and chance—in his business and professional activity. The one all-knowing Mind is his inspiration and safeguard.

We can overcome the fear of being misjudged by our superiors or by anyone. "He that judgeth me is the Lord" (I Cor. 4:4), said Paul. And learning to judge rightly, ourselves, puts us in tune with that truth. We can educate ourselves not to judge before the time, and not to think for others. Going deeper, we can know that the one Mind, which is Principle, does not misjudge or misunderstand. No one can really be known other than as he is known of God.

Through Christian Science we can be immune to magnifying the errors of management. Mary Baker Eddy, the Discoverer and Founder of Christian Science, asks, "When will the world cease to judge of causes from a personal sense of things, conjectural and misapprehensive!" (*Miscellaneous Writings*, p. 290). Of course we want to be keen. Holding to the truth of God and man we're led to see the errors using people, but we also go further— unsee them, that is, see them as unreal. Then we see the truth that is there, the truth that error is claiming to hide. Every business and profession offers us an opportunity to acknowledge the government of divine law.

Now, about promotion. Mrs. Eddy gives us a grand recipe for promotion in these words, "Happy are the people whose God is All-in-all, who ask only to be judged according to their works, who live to love" (*The First Church of Christ, Scientist, and Miscellany,* p. 127). We're all able to increase our sense of service in our positions.

Once again, no organization or human being can limit our progress or future, because no organization or human being can limit our thinking. Real promotion is the elevation of our own thought above a sense of evil as real. That's where promotion comes from; it lies in our own understanding of God. As the Psalmist said: "For promotion cometh neither from the east, nor from the west, nor from the south. But God is the judge: he putteth down one, and setteth up another" (Ps. 75:6, 7). Our improved thought will expand into expression. The result will transcend what we could think, ask for, or outline. Let's not forget that progress is God's law. We demonstrate it by accepting it.

Opportunity and ability go together in Science. If you have the opportunity to do a right assignment, God furnishes the ability with which to accomplish it. And, vice versa, if you have ability, you always have the opportunity to exercise it. You really exist at the standpoint of perfect receptivity to good— yes, at the standpoint of limitless intelligence and ability. Why is this so? It's true because you are the son of the all-knowing Mind, of omniscience itself. This means that you include all right ideas and the power to express them.

There is nothing outside God's government and harmonious control. Every activity is going on in divine Mind under God, the one perfect Principle, who judges and rewards righteously. His law is a law of continuous progress for all.

—*Milton Simon*

"THY YEARS SHALL HAVE NO END"

*Y*ears have been poetically but fearsomely described as great black oxen treading down and crushing all that is in their path. Through the centuries similar false concepts have haunted men and created a fear of time which seemingly fulfills itself in disease and disability. Yet accumulated time, in itself, is powerless to infect mankind with degenerative disorders; it is mankind's expectance and acceptance of such evils as real which seemingly bring them about. It is possible today, through the revelation of Christian Science, to correct such erroneous thinking by establishing the truth of man's spiritual nature and existence, and thus to maintain health, activity, and vigor despite passing years. Time cannot alarm or even affect one who increasingly understands Life as God, omnipotent, omnipresent Love.

This practical, demonstrable religion was discovered and founded by Mary Baker Eddy. She learned through consecrated, inspired study of the Bible that God's laws are as applicable today to meet the human need as they were throughout Biblical history. They are based on divine Principle and therefore are changeless and scientific. Both the patriarchs and the prophets, through their radical acceptance of God's omnipotence, attained a degree of longevity which would be considered incredible according to modern standards.

The great Master and Way-shower, Christ Jesus, attained the complete demonstration of deathless life in his resurrection and ascension through the understanding of his spiritual preexistence as the beloved Son of God. He said (John 8:58), "Before Abraham was, I am." And the acknowledgment of his divine sonship in his statement (John 10:30), "I and my Father are one," carried with it the understanding of his ageless being as the reflection of that Life which is God, the acceptance of his eternal possession of every quality and condition of immortality. He knew that to accept the belief of mortal birth is to come under the seeming penalty of mortality, death. For mortality is death, and to repudiate its apparent reality or identity is to approach the demonstration of eternal life.

The leading error concerning man is the belief that he was born, that his existence became clarified and established through the physical channels of conception, development, and birth. How clearly, how definitely does Mrs. Eddy expose this falsity in the following passage from *Science and Health with Key to the Scriptures* (p. 550): "The continual contemplation of existence as material and corporeal—as beginning and ending, and with birth, decay, and dissolution as its component stages—hides the true and spiritual Life, and causes our standard to trail in the dust. If Life has any starting-point whatsoever, then the great I AM is a myth. If Life is God, as the Scriptures imply, then Life is not embryonic, it is infinite." How important, then, that we lift our concept of existence from matter to Spirit, from corporeality to Soul, from belief to understanding. And how comforting it is to realize that no claim of mortal mind can interfere with the consecrated, humble desire to know Life as God.

False human thinking has constituted itself a framework of limitation within which capabilities, faculties, and accomplishments are imprisoned. But there can be no measurement for the manifestation of infinite Life; no limit set upon the expression of infinite Truth; no boundary for the reflection of infinite Mind.

The writer of the one hundred and second Psalm must have caught more than a glimpse of the divinity of Life, untrammeled by mortality, for he contrasts the unreal, transitory nature of mortality with the imperishable, unchanging glory of infinity, concluding with the triumphant cry (verse 27), "But thou art the same, and thy years shall have no end." Similarly, there can be no end of life for man, because man, created by God in His exact likeness, is as infinite, as eternal, as his Maker. For him, life is not doled out through the grudging measure of time; it is the consummately natural expression of eternity, the unfolding glory of being.

Man, the idea of Spirit, is a spiritual phenomenon. His source is God. Therefore he never comes upon the darkness of disease, disability, death, but always upon the radiance of eternal harmony, health, holiness. He is an emanation of God, Life. Proportionately as this great fact unfolds and develops in human consciousness will the infirmities of mortality diminish until they disappear.

There is no paralysis, no stagnation, no inactivity in matter. Mortal mind alone contains and perpetuates these falsities, and outlines them upon its own subjective state, which it has named matter.

To dissociate one's intelligence and existence from every phase of mortality is to gain freedom from mortal despotism and to experience the clarity of vision, the logic of Truth, the glory of being, which belong to every idea of Mind.

The study of Christian Science opens one's eyes to the recognition of Life as the sole authority of existence. Through this recognition one ceases to reach hopefully toward the future possibility of immortal life, and begins to rejoice in his present possession of immortality as the child of God. The real man, the man whom God creates, constitutes, and controls, is already free from every false concept of creation as material. He is an inhabitant of the realm of spiritual reality, continually expressing the nature of his heavenly Father in such qualities as joy, peace, health, wisdom, and so on.

Mrs. Eddy, herself an inspiring example of the health-bestowing, life-preserving power of divine Science, has this to say of human existence (*Science and Health*, p. 246): "Except for the error of measuring and limiting all that is good and beautiful, man would enjoy more than threescore years and ten and still maintain his vigor, freshness, and promise. Man, governed by immortal Mind, is always beautiful and grand. Each succeeding year unfolds wisdom, beauty, and holiness."

Let us cease then to measure and begin to enjoy immortality!

—*Kathryn Paulson*

TRUE HEALTH

A Christian Scientist had long enjoyed an almost uniform sense of good health, which he attributed to his understanding, gained through Christian Science, of God as the only Life, and which he took very much for granted; but the time came when he found it necessary to establish his sense of health on the sure foundation of Christianly scientific demonstration. The aggressive mental suggestions poured into thought: Your health has been undermined, you have lost your health, you may not recover, and so on. In blessed reassurance came the inspired words of Isaiah (59:19), "When the enemy shall come in like a flood, the spirit of the Lord shall lift up a standard against him." And so it proved.

Mary Baker Eddy, the Discoverer and Founder of Christian Science, writes in the Christian Science textbook, *Science and Health with Key to the Scriptures* (p. 297), "It is as necessary for a health-illusion, as for an illusion of sickness, to be instructed out of itself into the understanding of what constitutes health; for a change in either a health-belief or a belief in sickness affects the physical condition." A belief in health based on the illusion of health as a physical condition is no more stable or real than a belief in sickness, for both are built on the sands of human variableness and have no foundation in Truth.

What then is health, and where is it to be found? Christian Science reveals health as a condition of Mind, of God, Spirit, not of matter. Hence scientific health is spiritual, an emanation of God. It is found in an understanding of God and exists wholly apart from the supposititious conditions of matter. Health is associated with holiness; the words *health, holy,* and *whole* have the same Anglo-Saxon derivation.

Christ Jesus illustrated the spiritual nature of health. With simple naturalness the Gospels recount multitudes made whole through the tender ministrations of the great Physician. His word broke the mesmerism and set the captive free. To the man whom he healed of the palsy he said (Luke 5:20), "Man, thy sins are forgiven thee," showing that true health is akin to holiness, not merely an absence of physical bondage. Jesus demonstrated God's law as a law of Love, not a law of penalty; he recognized no secondary law as able to defy the divine law. He accepted no evidence of the physical senses, but refuted it on the ground that it is un-Godlike,

hence illegitimate and untrue. He knew that God is the only power, and that God, good, is as incapable of sending evil as He is of experiencing evil; hence, that God is not the author of sickness. To those who through steadfast adherence to his teachings became his disciples he promised (John 8:32), "Ye shall know the truth, and the truth shall make you free." Jesus never compromised with error. He never administered material remedies. He proved health to be always present and forever intact, waiting only to be revealed through an understanding of God.

Mrs. Eddy defines *health* thus (*Miscellaneous Writings*, p. 298): "The true consciousness is the true health." Let us examine this statement and see where it leads. Since God is Mind, there is but one Mind, hence there can be but one consciousness, namely, Mind's awareness of itself. Consciousness cannot cognize or experience that which is unlike God, because God knows and experiences nothing beyond Himself. Mrs. Eddy says (*Science and Health*, p. 276), "Man and his Maker are correlated in divine Science, and real consciousness is cognizant only of the things of God." Outside of infinity nothing exists. Consciousness, then, is infinite; it is Mind's awareness of itself as Life, as Soul, Spirit, Principle, Truth, and Love. Thus true consciousness, or health, is God's consciousness of Himself reflected in the harmony of His creation—God's consciousness or experience of unlimited Life, without beginning or end; of the transcendent beauty of Soul, unmarred by flaw or blemish; of the vibrant energy of Spirit, the invariability of Principle, the substance of Truth, the well-being of Love.

Health cannot fluctuate. Man is the manifestation of health, as inseparable from health as he is from God. Health can no more be lost than God can be. It is incorruptible, inexhaustible, sound. It can never break down, can never lapse into disease, can never be tainted. Man's being, the reflection of God's being, is without poison, without defect, without pain, perfect in strength and freedom of action. Being is the rhythm of Soul; hence every function of being is normal, painless, unlabored, regular. Being is incapable of congestion or stoppage, of inflammation or decay. There is no obstruction to health because there is no obstruction in consciousness. There is no paralysis, because Mind or consciousness is perpetual motion. "The true consciousness is the true health."

Health does not inhere in a physical body; it is not controlled by physical law, is not shaped by hereditary belief. Health is God's expression of harmony. Man has no health apart from God; hence God is responsible for man's health. Furthermore, since there is but one consciousness there is but one health, and it is always complete health, always good health. There is no partial health, because there is no partial consciousness, no partial Mind. There are no degrees of health; Mind or Life in every instance expresses itself fully. There is no deterioration, no decomposition in Mind. Consciousness never lapses into unconsciousness; health never lapses into disease.

Health never stagnates; it never grows old; it never wears out. It is not localized; it is infinite. There is not more health in one place than in another. Health is not subject to atmospheric conditions, to temperature, to altitudes. Climate has nothing whatever to do with health.

Since health is infinite, it is universal. Also, being infinite it has never been lost; therefore it does not have to be regained. Health is never uncertain. Man is not dependent on his health for his efficiency; being dependent alone upon God, man manifests the health which God expresses. Because man reflects infinity he is never the victim of exhaustion. The limitless capacities of Life never wear out, they never grow threadbare, they never slow up. Man can no more break down than God can; he is never prostrated, because Mind, his Mind or consciousness, is forever active, forever intelligent, forever free, forever expressing the buoyancy of Soul.

Health is not something to be theorized about; it is a spiritual fact which demands demonstration. Mrs. Eddy points out that the basis of all disease is fear, ignorance, or sin (see *Science and Health*, p. 411). Christ Jesus proved this, as a study of his healing works will show. All erroneous conditions are the result of false education. Thus certain diseases are deemed contagious, others fatal. In every case mortal mind maps out the course and pronounces the sentence, and the one infinite, ever-available remedy is pure Mind. God knows nothing of curable or incurable diseases. He knows no man who needs healing. He rejoices ever in His own unrestricted expression of good.

A little Christian Scientist, instructed in the Christian Science Sunday School in the sweet naturalness of good, went one day to visit a friend who was not a Christian Scientist. The little friend's mother opened the door and promptly sent the visitor away, saying that she would get sick if she came in, because her child was sick. With simple logic the little Christian Scientist later said to her mother: "But, Mother, if Alice is sick and I am well, why should I get sick from her? Why shouldn't she get well from me?" It was many years later when the little girl now grown to womanhood discovered the identical reasoning in Mrs. Eddy's article entitled "Contagion" in *Miscellaneous Writings* (see p. 229).

The sure foundation of health is the impregnable oneness of God and man, of Mind and its idea. Mind without idea would be a nonentity; idea without Mind would be an impossibility. Thus idea has no existence separate from Mind; it never gets outside of Mind; it has no substance other than Mind, no entity or ego apart from Mind. It were as impossible for pure Mind to evolve an impure idea as for pure Mind to hold within itself an idea capable of corruption or contamination. Thus health is inherent in God's idea, the idea which is forever showing forth the beauty of Soul and the holiness of Love. God's consciousness of His own allness is the only true consciousness, and this true consciousness is true health, the health that is forever intact.

—*L. Ivimy Gwalter*

THE TRUTH ABOUT ADVERSITY

*T*here was once an individual who refused to be discouraged. One thing after another in his human affairs "went wrong," as the saying is; one disaster after another came upon him, apparently unjustly and through no fault of his own; but no matter what happened, he kept his poise. In fact, his manner of dealing with each seeming adversity was such that he actually succeeded in turning it into a blessing not only to himself, but to all with whom he was associated. He evidently had unshakable faith in the ultimate triumph of right, this Hebrew lad Joseph, of long ago, whom the compelling hand of Love took from feeding his father's sheep to make of him the greatest influence for good in what was at that time the most powerful kingdom in the world. No matter how acute the condition became, he evidently made no complaint. No matter how hopeless the situation might seem, his courage did not fail. He simply trusted God, and did the best he could (see Gen. 37-45).

It is a beautiful story, and vibrant with interest to the Christian Scientist today, for it illustrates how every adverse circumstance, if taken rightly, can be turned into a new opportunity to prove the truth of the Scriptural saying that "all things work together for good to them that love God" (Rom. 8:28). Did his brethren, inflamed with envy and jealousy, cast him into a pit in the wilderness? It all worked together for good, for he was presently sold to merchantmen and carried into Egypt, which brought him just that much nearer to the great work of his life. True, he was only a slave there, but that did not dishearten him. All things were still working together for good, and he quietly went about his business, doing the best he could. The sudden transition from his simple home in the land of Canaan to the house of Potiphar, the rich Egyptian, did not confuse him, nor rob him of his poise. He performed the duties required of him in his master's household, undisturbed by the fact that he was a captive in an alien land, and untouched by the gross materiality about him.

This same fidelity of purpose, this same integrity of thought and conduct which had so aroused the hatred and envy of his brethren, once more enraged the carnal mind, and impersonal evil found a new channel through which it hoped to accomplish his downfall. On a false accusation he was thrown into prison. There is no record, however, that he indulged in self-pity, self-righteousness, resentment, or bitter condemnation, nor did he spend precious time in bemoaning his fate, so far as we know. He still believed in his God, and that all things were still working together for good. Did it seem to human sense that his usefulness was over, that his work had been taken from him? Not so. The work he had been doing had undoubtedly been taken from him, but that only meant that another work was just beginning. If he could no longer do the big things for his master, which he had been doing so faithfully and well, he could still do little things for his fellow prisoners, and do them just as faithfully and just as well. Perhaps he had already learned that it is not the size of the things done which counts so much, as the spirit in which they are done.

We know the rest of the story, how he was finally brought forth by one whom he had befriended in the prison to interpret a dream for the great Pharaoh himself, which so pleased the king that he was set free and placed in a position whereby he was able by his wisdom and sagacity to save countless thousands from hunger or starvation, among them his own father and his traitorous brethren. And how graciously he forgave his brethren, and pointed out to them that all things are in God's hand, even in the darkest hours of our lives! There was a perfect plan to be wrought out, and he and they were just a part of it. "Be not grieved," he told them tenderly, "nor angry with yourselves, that ye sold me hither: for God did send me before you to preserve life. ... So now it was not you that sent me hither, but God" (Gen. 45:5, 8).

Well for us today if, in the midst of a seeming affliction, we may echo these words that "it was not you that sent me hither, but God," thus establishing the eternal truth that the wrath of man shall praise Him! For we sometimes feel as if Joseph were not the only one who was ever sold "into Egypt," a helpless victim of envy, revenge, treachery, and cruelty. Yet we are told by our beloved Leader, Mary Baker Eddy, that "whatever envy, hatred, revenge— the most remorseless motives that govern mortal mind—whatever these try to do, shall 'work together for good to them that love God'" (*Miscellaneous Writings,* p. 10). Each stage of human experience through which Joseph passed, proved to be essential to the next step in his progress, and all were without exception along the line of spiritual advancement, although they appeared at the time to be exactly the opposite. If he had not been thrown into the pit, he would never, in all probability, have reached the land of Egypt. If he had never reached the land of Egypt, he would never have dwelt in Potiphar's house and incurred the enmity of one of its inmates. If this enmity had not occurred, he would not have been thrown into the prison in disgrace; and if he had not been placed in prison he would not have known one of its inmates, a fellow companion in misery, who afterwards, upon being released and restored to favor, remembered Joseph, and was the direct cause of his being brought before Pharaoh. If Pharaoh's attention had not thus been called to him, he would not have had the opportunity so to prove his wisdom beyond that of all the king's astrologers and soothsayers that he was exalted to the highest rank and power. And if he had not possessed this rank and power, he could not have been in a position to make a decree whereby not only Egypt but other nations were saved from seven years of famine, nor have brought about a reconciliation between himself and his brethren.

Like a continuous golden thread the omnipotence of good runs through the entire fabric of his various experiences, linking the different parts together into a complete whole. The poet Browning caught some vision of this divine continuity when he wrote, "On the earth, the broken arcs; in the heaven, a perfect round" (Robert Browning, "Abt Vogler," *The Oxford Book of English Mystical Verse*, eds. Nicholson and Lee, 1917).

The limited range of human vision can see only "the broken arcs" of the circle, the bits, the pieces, the detached portions, so to speak, of the entire plan, the "perfect round," but when we come to see more as God sees, we realize that each and every one was needed in order to make manifest that which was an established fact in Mind before the morning stars first sang together in joy.

One sometimes hears it said: "But why should all this come upon me? Why do I have all this trouble when I am trying so hard to do right?" Joseph was trying to do right, too, and yet it did not save him from the pit and the dungeon. Daniel was trying to do right, and yet he had to go into the lions' den. They were just new opportunities to prove in what direction their trust lay, whether in the omnipotence of good or in the boasted power of evil. It is safe to say that there is hardly a person in the world today who does not, at times, feel he has something to forgive. Perhaps even yet, strive as one may, a certain face comes back again and again upon his mental vision, or a certain set of

circumstances, which he would fain forget, intrudes itself upon his harmony. If so, let him find comfort in pondering the story of this man of long ago who accepted adversity so well, and trusted God so completely, even under the greatest stress of circumstances, that the wonder and the inspiration of it have come down to us through the lapse of all these dusty centuries.

Unpleasant and unjust and trying experiences come to every one of us, and they are easily accounted for, because as Christian Scientists we are constantly going against the current of popular thought, and when one rows his boat upstream and against the current he encounters more obstacles and goes more slowly than the one who is idly drifting downstream. But to float along with popular opinion and established precedent, is not to grow. Instead, let us say with the apostle, "…none of these things move me" (Acts 20:24). Not one of these things should shake our trust in God and His perfect plan, which, as yet, we may discern but faintly, but in which every one of us belongs. We must trust Him with these "broken arcs," these seemingly unattached incidents of daily experience, and realize that, even though we may seem to be cast into the deepest pit of loneliness, fear, and despair, all things are still working together for good. Love will never leave us comfortless, and already a friendly hand, yet unseen by us, may be reaching out towards us in the darkness. Do some of us feel that we are already slaves to wrong environment, held in subjection to materiality, placed in the stifling atmosphere of surroundings not conducive to spiritual growth and development, a veritable prison-house of limitation, thwarted effort, discouragement, frustration? These are only bringing new opportunities to prove that God is All-in-all, to trust more, to forgive more, to see the perfect man where sense testimony would see an imperfect mortal, to maintain the impersonality of evil, and to ask ourselves the question, "Do we yet understand how much better it is to be wronged, than to commit wrong?" (*Miscellaneous Writings*, p. 130). Then let us praise God for these lessons in patience, humility, unrequited service, unappreciated effort, hope deferred, forgiveness, charity, unselfed love. Suffering sense can see only the present moment, with its false conclusions drawn from material, finite testimony, but let it be ever remembered that "what is termed material sense can report only a mortal temporary sense of things, whereas spiritual sense can bear witness only to Truth" (*Science and Health with Key to the Scriptures*, p. 298).

"O thou afflicted, tossed with tempest, and not comforted"(Isa. 54:11), dry those unavailing, useless, unworthy tears, and look up. Lift your thought above "man's inhumanity to man," to realize more of the dear Father's great universal love, and His care for everything, the flowers, the stars, the birds, the little lambs asleep, the baby leaves just uncurling in the April sun. Would His love enfold all these in tenderest care, and yet forget you, His dear child? The hour will surely come when you will look back upon this present experience, which now seems so hard and cruel and unjust, and realize that it was really a blessing in disguise, in that it compelled you to loose your hold upon human help and turn more unreservedly to God as the supreme power, the one great All-in-all. You will at length realize that had it not come, you might not have so quickly reached the higher point of vision whereon you stand today; and as you look back upon it, and see how much it taught you, and how far along the heavenly way you are because of it, your heart will silently sing for joy, and you will find yourself whispering, as to someone very near, "Father, I thank thee."

—*Louise Knight Wheatley Cook*

Undisturbed

In one of his discourses Jesus told his disciples, "Hereafter I will not talk much with you: for the prince of this world cometh, and hath nothing in me" (John 14:30). Nothing in the world could disturb Jesus or turn him from the contemplation of the Christ, Truth, which animated him. He was conscious of God as He is, and of his own true selfhood in the likeness of the divine. He understood God to be eternal Life, the one all-inclusive, frictionless Being.

There is nothing outside of God that could encroach upon Him. If there were any element of discord in infinite Being, Life would ultimately spend itself. To be eternal, Life must be without any element of friction. This one undisturbable Being is eternally expressed by each one of us because man is the reflection of infinite Life and perfect Mind.

Individuals, then, are wrong when they believe that they are in possession of disquieting tendencies or undesirable traits and that little can be done about it. How erroneous to accept as belonging to God's child any sense of irritation! Neither receptivity to healing nor the power to heal others resides in an irritated, disturbed mentality. But in the consciousness that is uplifted and at peace the healing Christ, the power of God, is felt. So our goal is to understand and manifest our divine sonship through the tranquillity inherent in us and thus to demonstrate our immunity to anxiety and disturbance.

If we can be disturbed by certain circumstances or the actions of someone else, then is not our peace of mind in a precarious state? Is not this an indication, too, that there is need for us to correct our own consciousness until every tendency to be annoyed is conquered? Actually, not the situation itself, but our own sense of it is all that is disquieting.

God's man is not disturbed. Then what is irritated at the actions of another? Usually it is egotism, pride, or self-will, claiming existence in one's consciousness. Or it may be self-righteousness that is sometimes shocked at what it terms the enormity of error. When truth has been assimilated, one is governed by spiritual sense. Then error's pretense no longer deceives and upsets. Mortal mind has only its own erring concepts. When others seem to think wrongly about us, we know that they are thinking only of their own wrong concept of us. That, of course, in reality never touches, much less harms, us. The one undisturbable Mind governs all in peace and harmony. This Mind, the Mind of every individual, does not misunderstand, but ever loves its own ideas. As Jeremiah expresses it (29:11), "For I know the thoughts that I think toward you, saith the Lord, thoughts of peace, and not of evil, to give you an expected end."

Confronted by an untoward incident, mortal mind is apt to exclaim, "What happened?" It accepts the distressing circumstance as taking place and attempts to assign a material cause for it. Christian Science denies its occurrence. It handles the situation, not as a personal experience, but as animal magnetism attempting to hide the inviolate good that is always present. What seems to be disturbing does not exist in reality, for God's allness cannot be invaded. It seems real only to unenlightened thought. It is rectified, or eliminated, as the need may be, by our correction of our erring sense of it with the understanding that everything that has presence or existence is good.

We should scientifically handle as impersonal and as nonexistent the suggestion that we are erring mortals. We can see through evil's machinations to man's true selfhood, as never expressing any sort of imperfection. Indeed, we can be alert to every attempt of error to deceive and irritate. In our true being we are sensitive to good alone.

Nervousness and emotionalism—tension, grief, resentment, irritation—are suggestions of evil that would confuse and disturb. Individuals jeopardize their growth Spiritward when they contend for what they term their nature, their emotional tendencies, or their indulgences. To argue for them is to succumb to animal magnetism's attempt to retard healing. Erring emotions cannot cling to one who understands the real man. They have no power with which to fasten themselves onto one. But we have power from God to hold thought to good. The exercise of this true tenacity aids in destroying the false belief in erring emotional tendencies.

Today materia medica is claiming that many ailments are caused by nervous or emotional disturbances. Yet Truth destroys these tendencies as erring beliefs and also heals the discordant bodily conditions to which these agitated feelings seem to give rise. One should not accede to the erroneous supposition that it is wrong to thwart emotions. Even momentary indulgence prolongs, never ends, their suppositional existence. One does not become honest through stealing, nor can he demonstrate tranquillity through irritation. The slightest irritation is without justification in Truth.

Beliefs in nervousness and upsetting emotions come from the ignorant assumption that man is separated from God. False belief claims that he is a mortal, controlled by material nerves. The fact is that man is spiritual, eternally at one with God, Love, controlled by Him alone, and that he is forever expressing Love's uninvadable harmonious control. The truth which saves from the belief in weak, tired nerves, nervous prostration, false stimulation, and agitating emotions is the inseparability of divine Mind and its perfect idea, man.

Peace of mind is a pearl of great price that is not to be forfeited under the pressure of aggressive sense testimony. Let us ask ourselves, "Is there anything worth being disturbed about?" The evil of being disturbed is not just that we have allowed ourselves to be upset, but that we have succumbed to error's attempt to hide ever-present good from us. When one is conscious of man's unity with divine Love, he is undisturbed, poised, and ever at peace. He expresses the firmness and stability of Principle. His orderly, disciplined mentality is not only stable, but also active in its adherence to good.

In writing of the Christ, which Jesus so perfectly expressed, Mary Baker Eddy says in *Science and Health with Key to the Scriptures* (p. 26), "This Christ, or divinity of the man Jesus, was his divine nature, the godliness which animated him." The Christ is always acquainting us with our radiant, spiritual selfhood, and it reveals our indissoluble oneness, or unity, with God as ever satisfying and permanent. The recognition of this unity removes us from the influence of every upsetting suggestion and enables us to maintain an abiding consciousness of God's presence and love.

This consciousness includes nothing that can be disturbed, for it is a reflection of the undisturbable Mind, which is God. To thought so illumined these healing words of our Leader's glow with new spiritual meaning (*ibid.*, p. 306): "Undisturbed amid the jarring testimony of the material senses, Science, still enthroned, is unfolding to mortals the immutable, harmonious, divine Principle,—is unfolding Life and the universe, ever present and eternal."

—*Milton Simon*

WISER THAN SERPENTS

It may be said that all of the trouble in the world comes from failure to handle animal magnetism. Since it is the necessity of Christians to imitate the example of Christ Jesus, it follows that Christians have the inescapable duty of proving the unreality of the works of the devil. Now, the works of the devil, evil, may be said in a general way to be comprised in the supposititious activities of mortal mind. Only when the so-called human mind yields to divine wisdom, to the government of the one divine Mind, God, does it awaken from the mesmeric dream of evil thoughts and deeds. Christian Scientists, who are in a measure aroused from this hypnosis, are proportionately capable of overcoming evil in themselves and others.

Animal magnetism is a name for evil in its false claim to be and to do something; it is the belief of evil in action. Wherever a falsity claims to be exerting itself to be and to do, there is animal magnetism. In the Christian Science textbook, *Science and Health with Key to the Scriptures*, Mary Baker Eddy gives "animal magnetism" as a definition of *serpent* (p. 594).

The word *serpent* appears early in the Scriptures; and throughout both the Bible and *Science and Health* it is employed as the adequate type of evil. From the statement regarding it in Genesis, it has stood for what Paul defined as the "deceivableness of unrighteousness" (II Thess. 2:10). In Genesis 3:1 we are told, "Now the serpent was more subtil than any beast of the field which the Lord God had made," and the Scriptural narrative presents the qualities of the serpent as subtlety, duplicity, venom, adroitness, cunning, charm, fear, hate, anger, the counterfeit of wisdom.

The serpent is represented as engendering fear. It claims to terrorize, fascinate, and kill. It is supposed to produce and transmit poison. Its entire activity claims to be destructive; and this characteristic remands it to the realm of the unreal, to the sphere of the nonexistent, for that which is destructive or destructible cannot really continue even to seem to exist—it carries within itself the element of oblivion.

The one quality ascribed to the serpent that would seem to have reality is wisdom. To be sure, adroitness and charm have also better meanings, and when, together with wisdom, they are considered spiritually, they are properly attributable to the serpent of God's creating, of which Mrs. Eddy writes in *Science and Health*, "The serpent of God's creating is neither subtle nor poisonous, but is a wise idea, charming in its adroitness, for Love's ideas are subject to the Mind which forms them,—the power which changeth the serpent into a staff" (p. 515).

The use of the word *wisdom* as applied to the mortal mind sense of serpent is similar to Jesus' reference to the wisdom of this world. He said, "The children of this world are in their generation wiser than the children of light" (Luke 16:8). Here wisdom has more the qualities of prudence and discretion. Jesus commended these qualities, and said to his disciples, "Behold, I send you forth as sheep in the midst of wolves: be ye therefore wise as serpents, and harmless as doves" (Matt. 10:16).

In *Miscellaneous Writings*, Mrs. Eddy amplifies what the Master said at the time, by declaring that "the wisdom of a serpent is to hide itself" (p. 210). We are, then, to obey the injunction of the Master by hiding ourselves from error's inspection and action, which are always with intent to harm and destroy. Mrs. Eddy also declares in her *Message to The Mother Church for 1902*, "It is wise to be willing to wait on God, and to be wiser than serpents" (p. 17). Since the serpent here is a synonym of all active evil, or animal magnetism, we have need to be wiser than animal magnetism.

In the allegory of the Garden of Eden, the serpent is represented as talking to Eve. Mrs. Eddy reminds us that there is no such thing in animal life as a talking snake (*Science and Health*, p. 529). The talking serpent used Eve's tongue, for it had no ability to talk itself. Evil may even, fraudulently, take the livery of heaven. The serpent talked to Eve in terms of her own thinking and speech. Indeed, any evil belief comes to us in the guise of our own thought. It can come in no other way, since we see, feel, hear, touch, and taste only what we believe. Thus all these evil things depend for their seeming reality upon our acceptance of them at the behest of mortal mind.

Now the question arises, How can a talking serpent hide itself? Will not its speech inevitably betray it even if behind a camouflage of words? According to Paul, "the god of this world" (II Cor. 4:4)—the devil, evil, animal magnetism, the original talking serpent—is "dishonesty, … craftiness, … handling the word of God deceitfully" (*ibid.,* 4:2). Beware the smooth talker, who hides behind the words of truth, the lying maker of the venom of malice and mischief. There is little to choose between the venom producer and the venom vendor, carrying and spreading the poison of gossip, scandal mongering, idle talk, malicious criticism.

"The wisdom of a serpent is to hide itself"; and because the serpents of error come to us in the guise of thought, and can come in no other way, therefore the serpent hides itself in our own thinking. We must seek for it there. The animal magnetism outside our own consciousness can never harm us. "The wisdom of a serpent is to hide itself" by masquerading as good, created reality. For this reason, the serpent is a type of hypocrisy with all "deceivableness of unrighteousness."

This animal element, which claims to be inherent in mortals, impels them to all evil in the name of good. Animal subtleties are deceived and deceiving, but to themselves alone. Paul wrote to the Corinthians, "I fear, lest by any means, as the serpent beguiled Eve through his subtilty, so your minds should be corrupted from the simplicity that is in Christ" (*ibid.,* 11:3). This simplicity in Christ, Truth, enables one to break the mesmeric charm of matter's seemingly pleasant aspects and to antidote the hypnotic virus of matter's ugly phases.

In displaying its so-called wisdom, the serpent hides itself in the most effective place for hiding, namely, a hole. The superficial student hesitates or stops short at the hole of the serpent. He loves to think of God as Love, but he dislikes to stir up a nest of serpents. He will not handle animal magnetism. He either does not see the error or, seeing it, does not want to or will not deny it, reverse it, and reject it.

The true Scientist boldly turns the serpent out of its hole. He does this with the wisdom of God and not with his own human mentality, however. Thus he emulates our Leader's counsel and example "to be wiser than serpents." "To be wiser than serpents" is to employ the wisdom of God, the one divine Mind, in bringing the serpent out of its hiding place, or hole, handling it, and taking away its sting. Thus handled, that is, reversed with Truth, the lie, or serpent, becomes a staff on which to lean (*Science and Health,* p. 321). Note that to be wiser than a serpent is to employ the wisdom of God, not of oneself. No one can, of his own belief in mortal mind or will, uncover error. The true Scientist lets Truth uncover error.

The lie uncovered, the student should destroy it but only by replacing it with the truth. All animal magnetism is a supposititious reversal of the divine activity of Christ, or Truth. As has been previously stated, the serpent, when reversed in Science, becomes a staff on which to lean. If we allow Truth to uncover error, we shall find the serpent replaced by a staff. We must be active in allowing Truth to uncover the lie; we must be insistent and persistent. God must do this; but we must see to it that we are witnesses to Truth's activity.

Jesus said, "I am not come to destroy, but to fulfil" (Matt. 5:17). May not this be taken to mean, I am not come to destroy reality, but to restore it to consciousness? If we handle the serpent of materialism with the wisdom of God, we shall realize, proportionately to our right activity, the allness of Spirit and spiritual things. Christian Science is not destructive, but restorative. Not even the serpent itself is lost in reversion, but it thus becomes a type of true wisdom.

All too often the hole of the asp is to be found in one's own bosom. Such a hiding place seems most immune from attack. People are usually more willing to invade the nest of error in another's thought and heart, and sometimes without the wisdom of God, than to dig out the nests of evil within their own thinking, a process which requires greatest courage.

It is natural for a Christian Scientist to handle serpents. Jesus said of his disciples that they should do so unharmed: and a Christian Scientist who does not handle animal magnetism, and handle it with divine omnipotence, is not a genuine disciple of Christ or a worthy follower of his Leader. It is unnatural for a Christian Scientist to ignore the serpents or their hiding places. One should use discretion and be sure of his ability to accomplish what he would do for Christ.

How can one be sure of his ability, capacity, and competency? By preparedness. If the student does his daily work effectively against animal magnetism, he will find that the work on any specific case will become more and more incidental. He should remember that while the rattlesnake heralds his offensive, more serpents are quiet, striking without warning; hence the necessity to be impervious and immune to their poison. The antidote for all serpent bites is spiritual thinking and living; for spiritual sense alone can immunize against the mesmerism of the beliefs of matter.

"To be wiser than serpents" is also to be undeceived by hidden sin. Conversely, we should be "wise as serpents" in hiding our aims and plans from mortal mind. The serpent is wise enough to attempt to hide its venom, its presence and purpose. We should be wise to detect, attack, and destroy the serpent with its supposititious virus. We should cultivate perception, initiative, and spontaneity in handling evil. Our Leader tells us that the illusion of Moses regarding the serpent lost its power to alarm him when he reached out and conquered his fear (*Science and Health*, p. 321).

In one of the pictures in *Christ and Christmas* Mrs. Eddy places the serpent behind the woman. Jesus said, "Get thee behind me, Satan" (Luke 4:8). King Hezekiah sang, "Thou hast cast all my sins behind thy back" (Isa. 38:17). Paul declared that he was intent upon "forgetting those things which are behind" (Phil. 3:13). A lie is never true; the unreal does not exist. Jesus knew this and feared not animal magnetism; otherwise, he could not have put the serpent behind him. But note! Jesus commanded Satan, the lie, to get behind him. He handled the serpent of animal magnetism, but as nothing and with the power of Truth.

Nothing can replace the Christ and spiritual consciousness. Beware the serpent of materialism, hiding its purpose to destroy both individual lives and usefulness and the existence and usefulness of the movement of Christian Science by magnifying the supposititious material in the place of or in the guise of the spiritual. There is no kinship between the material and the spiritual. If we protect evil beliefs by our approval and indulgence, tacitly or openly, the consequent multiplication of the serpent's progeny will increase our pains and regrets. If we concede room to one devil, we may find seven others come to share its abode in our consciousness.

These serpents, or animal magnetism, are not people or things, even though mortal mind does claim to operate as mortal men and things. These serpents are, one and all, just false concepts, material beliefs. The serpent we handle for ourselves we at the same time handle impersonally for others—indeed for all mankind—because Christ, Truth, which heals and saves anybody, truly heals and saves everybody. Can we not visualize that happy day when "they shall take up serpents; and if they drink any deadly thing, it shall not hurt them" (Mark 16:18)? And why? Because they shall be "wise as serpents," yea, they shall be "wiser than serpents." Then "they shall not hurt nor destroy in all my holy mountain: for the earth shall be full of the knowledge of the Lord, as the waters cover the sea" (Isa. 11:9).

—*John M. Tutt*

NOTES

NOTES

INDEXES

Partial Subject Index

Partial Subject Index

Partial Subject Index

PARTIAL SUBJECT INDEX

Partial Subject Index

PARTIAL SUBJECT INDEX

Partial Subject Index

This subject index is provided simply as a starting point—it is not comprehensive nor conclusive.

Author Index

Publication Date Index

⁖

PUBLICATION DATE INDEX

Publication Date Index

NOTES

NOTES

ABOUT MARY BAKER EDDY

Mary Baker Eddy, the Discoverer and Founder of Christian Science, was healed of life-threatening injuries by praying and reading her Bible, including the account in the Gospel of Mark about Christ Jesus healing a man of palsy. Following her healing, she committed her life to understanding how Jesus healed. She explained her discovery of Christian Science in her book, published in 1875, called *Science and Health with Key to the Scriptures*. This book has opened the inspired meaning of the Bible to millions. To help spread this message of healing, Mrs. Eddy founded The Church of Christ, Scientist, in 1879 "…to commemorate the word and works of our Master, which should reinstate primitive Christianity and its lost element of healing" (*Church Manual*, p. 17). She began publishing magazines and eventually a newspaper, to enable the Christ-message to reach a wider audience.

For more information about Mary Baker Eddy, please visit
www.marybakereddylibrary.org